fat-free
BARBECUES

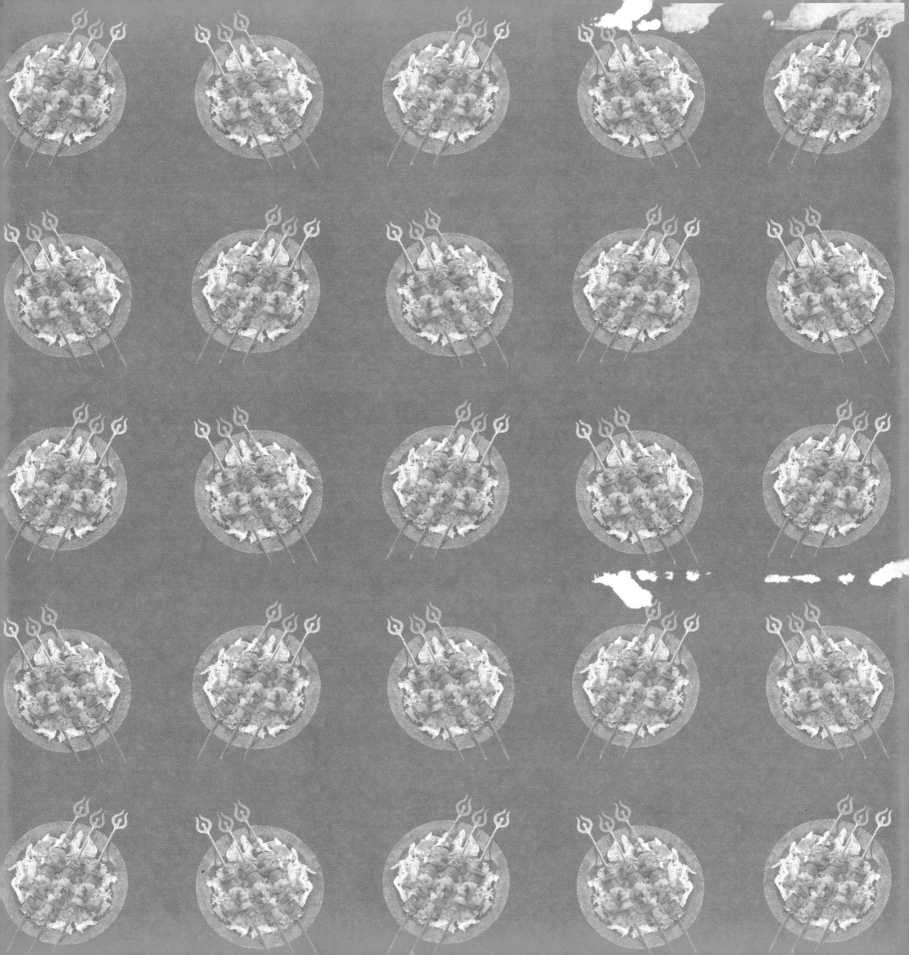

fat-free
BARBECUES

CONSULTANT EDITOR
MADELINE WESTON

LORENZ BOOKS

First published in 1999 by Lorenz Books

© Anness Publishing Limited 1999

Lorenz Books is an imprint of
Anness Publishing Limited
Hermes House
88–89 Blackfriars Road
London SE1 8HA

This edition distributed in Canada by Raincoast Books,
8680 Cambie Street, Vancouver, British Columbia, V6P 6M9

This edition published in 1999 for Index

ISBN 0 7548 0109 8

A CIP catalogue record for this book is available from the British Library.

Publisher: Joanna Lorenz
Project Editor: Zoe Antoniou
Editorial Reader: Richard McGinlay
Production Controller: Mark Fennell
Designer: Ian Sandom
Photographers: Karl Adamson, David Armstrong, Steve Baxter, James Duncan, Michelle Garrett, Amanda
Heywood, David Jordan, Don Last, William Lingwood, Patrick McLeavey, Thomas Odulate and Juliet Piddington
Recipes: Catherine Atkinson, Janet Brinkworth, Kit Chan, Jacqueline Clark, Carole Clements, Patrizia Diemling,
Nicola Diggins, Matthew Drennan, Joanna Farrow, Christine France, Silvana Franco, Sarah Gates, Rosamund Grant,
Janine Hosegood, Shehzad Husain, Christine Ingram, Peter Jordan, Manisha Kanani, Masaki Ko, Gilly Love, Lesley
Mackley, Sue Maggs, Sallie Morris, Annie Nichols, Anne Sheasby, Jenny Stacey, Liz Trigg, Steven Wheeler, Judy
Williams and Elizabeth Wolf-Cohen

For all recipes, quantities are given in both metric and imperial measures and, where appropriate, measures are
also given in standard cups and spoons. Follow one set, but not a mixture,
because they are not interchangeable.

Please use medium-sized eggs unless otherwise stated.

Printed and bound in Hong Kong

1 3 5 7 9 10 8 6 4 2

CONTENTS

INTRODUCTION

The barbecue is one of those special ways of entertaining that appeals to virtually everyone. Food that is cooked over charcoal and eaten *al fresco* always seems to have twice the flavour of the same dish cooked under the grill in the kitchen. The tantalizing aroma of chargrilled chicken, vegetables or fruit whets the appetite in a way that absolutely nothing else can.

However, health concerns have often gone by the wayside when cooking over coals – a lot of people think that food must be liberally doused with oil to keep it moist in the heat of the charcoal. Most of us know that reducing our intake of fat (especially saturated fats) also reduces our risk of heart disease. But up to now, there has been little encouragement for the health-conscious to extend low-fat cooking to the barbecue.

The recipes collected here show how you can cook spicy grills of meat, poultry and fish, flavoured with easy marinades – without losing any of the flavour or tenderness. Indeed, the technique of marinating is designed both to flavour and to tenderize – and you will learn how to cut down oil to the bare minimum and, on occasion, to abandon it altogether.

Vegetarian dishes, refreshing salsas, and accompanying salads are all included in this selection, as well as chargrilled fruit desserts and cooling fruit drinks and ices. All the recipes are so low in fat as to be virtually fat-free, but you will be delighted to find that your barbecues are more delicious than ever.

Choosing a Barbecue

There is a huge choice of ready-made barbecues on the market and it's important to choose one that suits your needs. First decide how many people you usually cook for and where you are likely to use the barbecue. For instance, do you usually have barbecues just for the family, or are you going to have barbecue parties for lots of friends? Once you've decided on your basic requirements, you will be able to choose between the different types more easily.

Hibachi barbecues
These small cast-iron barbecues originated in Japan – the word hibachi translates literally as "firebowl". They are inexpensive, easy to use and transportable. Lightweight versions are now made in steel or aluminium.

Disposable barbecues
These will last for about an hour, and are a convenient way of cooking for picnic-style barbecues, for example, or for dealing with low quantities of small pieces of food.

Portable barbecues
These are usually quite light and fold away easily to fit into a car boot so that you can take them on picnics. Some are even small enough to fit into a rucksack.

Brazier barbecues
These open barbecues are suitable for use on a patio or in the garden. Most have legs or wheels and it's a good idea to check that the height suits you. The grill area can vary in size and the barbecue may be round or rectangular. It's useful to choose one that has a shelf attached to the side. Other extras may include an electric, battery-powered or clockwork spit; choose one on which you can adjust the height of the spit. Many have a hood, which comes in useful as a windbreak.

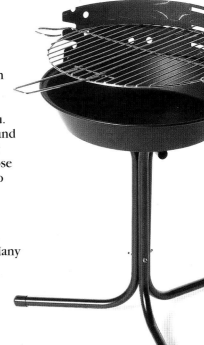

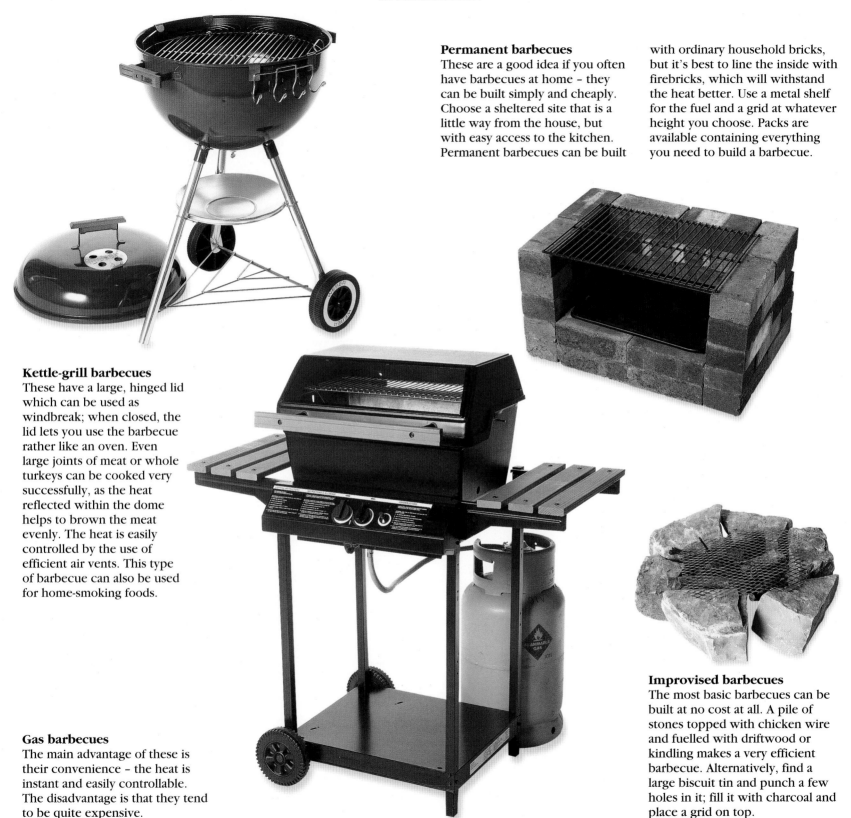

Permanent barbecues

These are a good idea if you often have barbecues at home – they can be built simply and cheaply. Choose a sheltered site that is a little way from the house, but with easy access to the kitchen. Permanent barbecues can be built with ordinary household bricks, but it's best to line the inside with firebricks, which will withstand the heat better. Use a metal shelf for the fuel and a grid at whatever height you choose. Packs are available containing everything you need to build a barbecue.

Kettle-grill barbecues

These have a large, hinged lid which can be used as windbreak; when closed, the lid lets you use the barbecue rather like an oven. Even large joints of meat or whole turkeys can be cooked very successfully, as the heat reflected within the dome helps to brown the meat evenly. The heat is easily controlled by the use of efficient air vents. This type of barbecue can also be used for home-smoking foods.

Gas barbecues

The main advantage of these is their convenience – the heat is instant and easily controllable. The disadvantage is that they tend to be quite expensive.

Improvised barbecues

The most basic barbecues can be built at no cost at all. A pile of stones topped with chicken wire and fuelled with driftwood or kindling makes a very efficient barbecue. Alternatively, find a large biscuit tin and punch a few holes in it; fill it with charcoal and place a grid on top.

Types of Fuel

If you have a gas or electric barbecue, you will not need to buy extra fuel, but most other barbecues use charcoal or wood. Whatever type of barbecue you have, choose good-quality fuel, and always store it in a dry place.

Woodchips or herbs
These are designed to be added to the fire to impart a pleasant aroma to the food. They must be soaked in order to make them last longer. Scatter them straight on to the coals during cooking, or place them on a metal tray under the grill rack. Packs of hickory or oak chips are easily available, or you can simply scatter twigs of juniper, rosemary, thyme, sage or fennel over the fire for a similarly striking effect.

Lumpwood charcoal
This is usually made from softwood, and comes in lumps of varying size. It is easier to ignite than briquettes, but tends to burn up faster.

Coconut-shell charcoal
This is not widely available, but it makes a good fuel for small barbecues. It's best used on a fire grate with little holes, as the small pieces tend to fall through the gaps.

Self-igniting charcoal
This is lumpwood charcoal or briquettes, treated with a flammable substance that catches light very easily. It's important to wait until the ignition agent has burned off before you actually cook food over it, or the smell may taint the food.

Charcoal briquettes
These are useful as they burn for a long time with the minimum of smell and smoke. They can, however, take time to ignite.

Wood
Hardwoods such as oak, apple, olive and cherry are best for barbecues, as they burn slowly with a pleasant aroma. Softwoods, however, tend to burn too fast and give off sparks and smoke, so they are unsuitable for most barbecues. Wood fires need constant attention to make sure that they keep an even and steady heat.

Safety Tips

Barbecuing is a perfectly safe method of cooking if it's done sensibly – use these simple guidelines as a basic checklist to safeguard against accidents. If you have never organized a barbecue before, keep your first few events as simple as possible, with just one or two types of food. When you have mastered the technique of cooking on a barbecue you can start to become more ambitious. Soon you will progress from simple burgers for two or three people to meals for large outdoor parties with all your family and friends.

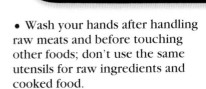
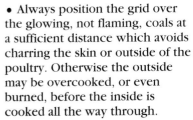

• Make sure the barbecue is sited on a firm surface and is stable and level before lighting. Once the barbecue is lit, make sure that it is not moved.

• Keep the barbecue sheltered from wind, and keep it well away from trees and shrubs.

• Always follow the manufacturer's instructions for your barbecue, as there are some barbecues that use only one type of fuel.

• Don't try to hurry the fire – some fuels may take quite a time to build up heat. Never pour flammable liquid on to the barbecue. This is very dangerous.

• Keep children (and pets) away from the fire and always make sure that the cooking is supervised by adults.

• Light the barbecue at least 30 minutes before cooking. Put food on it after the flames have died down to avoid too much burning, which can be harmful.

• Keep all raw foods that are yet to be cooked away from those foods that are already cooked and ready to eat. This is to prevent any possibility of the food becoming cross-contaminated.

• Make sure meats such as burgers, sausages and poultry are thoroughly cooked. Test by piercing the thickest part of the flesh: the juices should run clear and the flesh should not have any trace of pink.

• Wash your hands after handling raw meats and before touching other foods; don't use the same utensils for raw ingredients and cooked food.

• Always position the grid over the glowing, not flaming, coals at a sufficient distance which avoids charring the skin or outside of the poultry. Otherwise the outside may be overcooked, or even burned, before the inside is cooked all the way through.

• In case the fire should get out of control, you should have a bucket of sand and a water spray at the ready, with which to douse the flames. It's always better to be prepared than sorry.

• Keep a first-aid kit handy. If anyone does get burned, hold the burn under cold running water straight away.

• Trim any excess fat away from meat. Fat is not only unhealthy – it can also cause dangerous flare-ups if too much of it drips on to the hot fuel.

• Use long-handled barbecue tools, such as forks, tongs and brushes, for turning and basting food. Keep some oven gloves handy (preferably the extra-long type) in order to protect your hands from the heat.

Above: Keep all perishable foods cold and covered, in a cold box or bag until needed.
Left: Take care that marinades and oils are not spilt on the fire when brushing food.

Barbecue Tools and Equipment

Special barbecue tools are by no means essential, and you can often substitute them for what you already have at home. However, many of them actually make the job easier and often safer. The following are some of the best ones on the market.

Long-handled barbecue tools
These should include a pair of tongs, a fork and a flat slice for turning and lifting foods. Choose tools with wooden or heatproof handles, so they do not get too hot to hold.

Long-handled basting brushes
These are useful both for basting food and for oiling the grill rack. Choose those with real bristles, rather than nylon, which could melt or burn in use.

Skewers
For kebabs, flat metal skewers are good, particularly with meats, as they conduct the heat well; many have long heatproof handles or even hand-shields. Bamboo and wooden skewers are inexpensive and disposable. They're good for all types of food, but should be soaked in water before use to prevent them burning.

Hinged wire racks
These are useful for cooking and turning delicate items, such as whole fish, to prevent them from breaking up.

Oven gloves
Thick oven gloves or a cloth will protect your hands from the fire. Make sure that you choose well-padded cloth gloves – not thin ones which will not do the job.

Apron
An apron will protect you and your clothes from the fire and spattering food. It should be made from heavy-duty cotton, rather than plastic-coated.

Meat thermometer
A good thermometer will give a reading of the inside temperature of a large joint of meat. Take care not to touch the bone or the spit when you insert it, or you may get a false reading.

Chopping board
Use a heavy wooden or plastic board for cutting up food. Use different boards for meat to avoid cross-contamination.

Knife
Use a good sharp knife and again avoid cross-contamination by using a different one for meat.

Water spray
Similar to the type used for spraying house plants, this is useful for cooling the fire or dousing flames if it gets too hot.

Stiff wire brush
Use this or an abrasive pad and scraper to clean grill racks after cooking. Use with a detergent or a special spray-on barbecue cleaner. It is easier to clean the racks if they have been soaking.

oven glove

apron

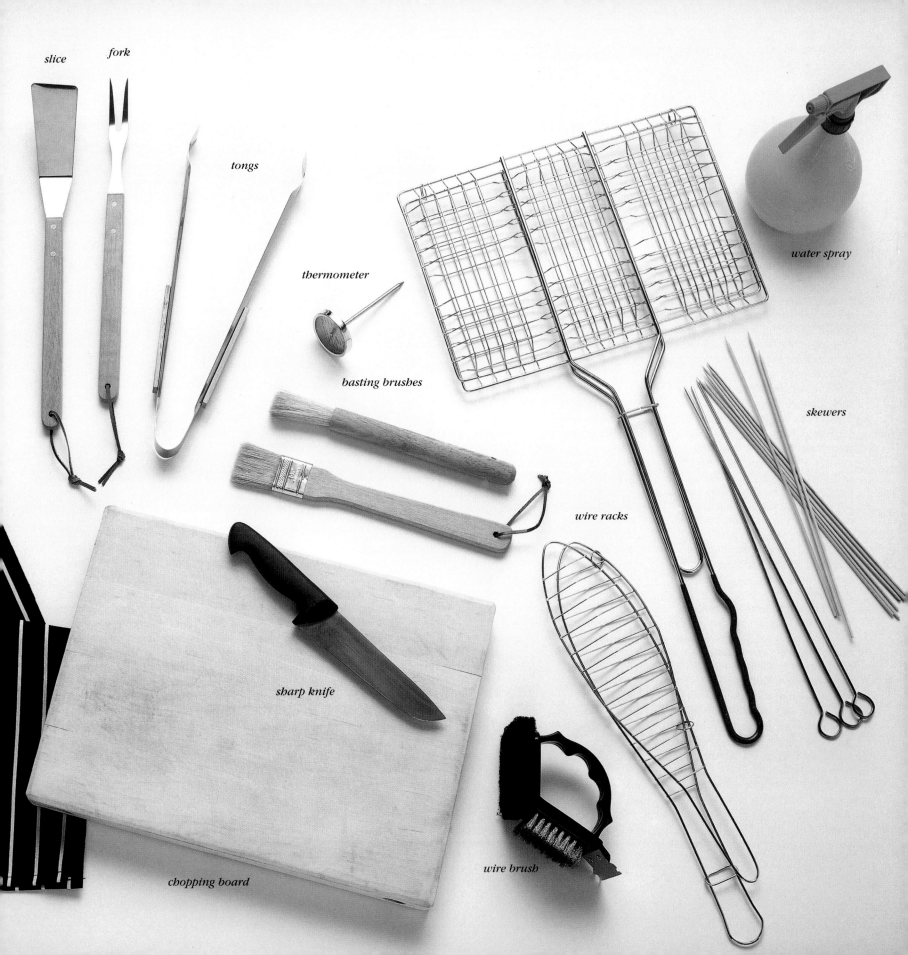

slice

fork

tongs

thermometer

basting brushes

water spray

skewers

wire racks

sharp knife

chopping board

wire brush

Cooking Fat-free Barbecues

Barbecuing can provide a very healthy and delicious way to cook food. However, it is the types of food that you choose to prepare and the ingredients used in marinating and basting them which will determine whether the fat content of your meal is high or low.

Eating a low-fat diet

A low-fat diet plays an important part in any healthy lifestyle. The amount of fat that we consume is affected by two main factors – the type of foods we eat most often and the way in which we prepare and cook them.

Barbecuing and grilling are the healthiest ways to cook, particularly because a certain amount of fat within the food will drip away during the cooking process. This method takes you halfway towards eating a low-fat diet. The second factor, the type of foods we eat, also plays a crucial role in determining whether your meal is healthy or not, so make sure you choose your ingredients well.

It is useful to know something about different fats before we can make changes to the way we eat. Some types are more harmful than others but a little fat is essential for a healthy diet. Knowledge of the different types of fat that exist in food will help you to choose not only what foods you barbecue but also the ingredients that will be used in your marinades.

It is important, however, that fat is not entirely eliminated from our diets – it is neither possible, nor healthy. Therefore, the definition of "fat-free" for the purpose of this book is a meal containing 5 g or less of fat.

• Saturated fats

These include butter and meat fat, which are solid at room temperature, and are thought to be a major factor in the development of heart disease.

• Monounsaturated fats

These are, in fact, thought to possibly help reduce the blood cholesterol level. They are found in olive oil, rapeseed oil, some nuts, oily fish and avocado pears.

• Polyunsaturated fats

These fats are found in some soft margarines and sunflower oil, and experts believe they should be eaten in moderation.

Nutritionists recommend that total daily fat consumption should not exceed 30 per cent of a person's daily calories. Saturated fat should be 10 per cent or less. It is important to cut down on fats, particularly saturated ones.

Choosing food for barbecues

Meat and poultry must be selected carefully. Red meats, such as lamb and beef, are particularly high in saturated fats and must be avoided, or at least kept to a minimum. Chicken and turkey are the ideal meats to cook, either in pieces or on skewers. Try to remove the skin from these meats as, by doing this, you are virtually halving the fat content of your meal.

Fish and prawns are wonderful when cooked on the barbecue. Choose white fish such as cod, swordfish or monkfish, rather than oily fish such as sardines.

Vegetables can be used to make equally delicious kebabs that are very low in fat. You could place corn-on-the-cob and potatoes wrapped in foil on the barbecue. Squares of tofu, or bean curd, make a great meat substitute which is very low in fat.

Marinating and basting

Choose your marinade ingredients with care. If you use oil, choose olive oil but try to replace most of it with other ingredients such as citrus juices or fat-free yogurts mixed with spices, to create some exciting and varied flavours.

It is important to baste the food with the marinade to keep it moist but do this sparingly, so you are not replacing oil which has already dripped away. Brush once just before you turn the food during cooking. If the food becomes dry, squeeze on a little citrus juice to keep it moist.

Above: Vegetable and plant oils and some margarines are high in polyunsaturates.
Left: Brush only a little oil on to food before barbecuing, or replace the oil with a fat-free marinade or citrus juices.

Tips for reducing the fat and not the flavour

It is possible to make the most delicious and exciting yet fat-free barbecues for your family and friends if you keep to some basic rules. There are in fact so many different foods you can cook and so many different ways to flavour them that the end result will always be delectable, if you are imaginative with your ingredients.

● Herbs, spices and crushed garlic can be rubbed into skinless chicken pieces before cooking; if you are cooking in the skin (to remove later) pierce the skin with a knife and insert the flavourings snugly underneath.

● Strew the coals with herbs, such as rosemary sprigs, to allow a subtle aroma to seep into the meat as it cooks.

● Make marinades of wine, cider, vinegar, lemon or lime juice to provide liquid in place of large amounts of oil. Marinate skinned or slashed chicken pieces in the fridge for at least 30 minutes to flavour and tenderize them.

● Sprinkle finely chopped shallots, onions or spring onions over poultry pieces for a particularly tangy taste.

● Before cooking, spread chicken breasts with prepared mustard marinades to moisten and add piquant flavour.

● Serve barbecued chicken with a salsa or relish, made from a selection of finely chopped fruit or vegetables, spring onions and chopped fresh herbs. This will add flavour to pitta bread kebabs.

● Fish only needs a short marinating time – if it is left too long the acid in the marinade will start to "cook" the flesh. Seafood such as squid, however, can be marinated for up to an hour to tenderize, and only needs very quick cooking over a high heat.

● Barbecue fish in its skin. This helps to keep it moist and easier to skin after cooking.

● When using fromage frais or yogurt in marinades or dips, use reduced fat, low-fat and fat-free versions. Such marinades create a succulent thick coating.

● A marinade made from low-fat yogurt and flavoured with Indian pastes, garlic and herbs, will adhere to chicken pieces better than a liquid marinade, which tends to drip off. It is also a most effective tenderizer.

● If you want to barbecue larger pieces of poultry, such as a whole bird, make a loose "hood" of foil to reflect the heat back, so that it is cooked from both sides. This also prevents drying and reduces the need for basting.

● Don't forget that how you serve your grilled food will also influence the fat content. Choose salads with light dressings and fat-free dips, together with wholemeal rolls and pitta breads as an accompaniment, for a healthy and substantial meal.

● If you have to use oil, choose olive, corn, sunflower, soya, rapeseed and peanut oils, which are low in saturates. Use the minimum amount for brushing or in marinades, and make up the difference with lemon juice, which is a natural tenderizer.

● Cook small vegetables, jacket potatoes or fish in foil parcels. Add citrus-based marinades to fish and vegetables to add flavour.

Below: Use spices such as (clockwise from top) green cardamom, mixed peppercorns, chillies, ground turmeric, cayenne pepper, caraway seeds and cinnamon sticks.

Fat-free Marinades

The type of marinade you use for barbecuing affects both the flavour and fat content of your food. Here is a delicious selection of more unusual ideas for you to try that are fat-free.

Keeping the flavour

Marinades are used to add flavour, moisten and tenderize foods, particularly meat, poultry and fish. Marinades usually contain citrus fruit juices or vinegar, but you can add all kinds of ingredients to create any kind of flavour; savoury or sweet, hot and spicy or fruity and fragrant. Experiment with more unusual combinations, such as cinnamon and cloves in red wine, or orange juice with cracked peppercorns.

In general, if the fat content of the food is very low, you'll need a little oil in the marinade. Chicken breast or white fish need some oil, but you can keep this to a minimum by replacing most of the oil with other ingredients such as fat-free yogurt.

To marinate, combine the ingredients together and mix with any poultry or meat. Cover and chill (this is not so important for vegetables). Use the times given in the recipes as your guide – marinating for too long may spoil delicate fish, but too short a time may mean that the flavours have not been absorbed. Tough meat or poultry can be marinated overnight. Use just a little to baste once during cooking, to keep the food moist.

GINGER AND LIME MARINADE
For meat, poultry or fish.

finely grated rind of 1 lime
juice of 1 lime
15 ml/1 tbsp olive oil
15 ml/1 tbsp green cardamom pods, seeded and crushed
2.5 cm/1 in piece fresh root ginger, peeled and grated
1 large garlic clove, crushed

BASIC BARBECUE MARINADE
This can be used for meat or fish.

1 garlic clove, crushed
15 ml/1 tbsp sunflower or olive oil
45 ml/3 tbsp dry sherry
30 ml/2 tbsp Worcestershire sauce
30 ml/2 tbsp dark soy sauce
freshly ground black pepper

HONEY CITRUS MARINADE
This is good with chicken or fish.

finely grated rind and juice of 1 lime, 1 lemon and ½ small orange
15 ml/1 tbsp sunflower oil
30 ml/2 tbsp clear honey
15 ml/1 tbsp soy sauce
5 ml/1 tsp Dijon mustard
freshly ground black pepper

YOGURT SPICE MARINADE
For meat, poultry or fish.

150 ml/¼ pint/⅔ cup low-fat natural yogurt
1 small onion, finely chopped
1 garlic clove, crushed
5 ml/1 tsp finely chopped fresh root ginger
5 ml/1 tsp ground coriander
5 ml/1 tsp ground cumin
2.5 ml/½ tsp ground turmeric

HERB MARINADE
This is good for meat, poultry or fish.

120 ml/4 fl oz/½ cup dry white wine
15 ml/1 tbsp olive oil
30 ml/2 tbsp lemon juice
30 ml/2 tbsp finely chopped fresh herbs, such as parsley, thyme, chives or basil
freshly ground black pepper

RED WINE MARINADE
Good with red meats and game.

150 ml/¼ pint/⅔ cup dry red wine
15 ml/1 tbsp olive oil
15 ml/1 tbsp red wine vinegar
2 garlic cloves, crushed
2 dried bay leaves, crumbled
freshly ground black pepper

Basic Timing Guide

It is important, particularly when cooking on the barbecue, to check that food is properly cooked. The timing chart offers a rough guide to cooking times for different foods, but always test to make sure it is cooked through before serving, if unsure.

Basic timing guide for barbecue cooking

Accurate timings for barbecuing are difficult to judge because the heat will vary according to the size and type of the barbecue, the type of fuel, and the height of the grill from the fire. Cooking times will also be affected by the thickness of the food and its position on the grill.

Always test the food carefully to make sure it is thoroughly cooked. Chicken should be cooked until the juices are clear and the flesh shows no trace of pink. Fish should be cooked until it is just opaque throughout, and no longer. Most foods need turning only once, but small items such as kebabs may need to be turned more frequently, to prevent them from burning.

The easiest way to regulate the heat is to adjust the height of the grill; some barbecues have air vents which also control the heat. For a medium heat, the rack should be about 10 cm/4 in from the coals. Raise the rack to obtain a lower heat, and lower the rack for a very high heat. Take care not to allow your food to char.

Type of Food	Weight or Thickness	Heat	Cooking Time (Total)
Chicken			
whole	1.5 kg/3½ lb	spit	1–1¼ hours
quarters, leg or breast		medium	30–35 minutes
boneless breasts		medium	10–15 minutes
drumsticks		medium	25–30 minutes
kebabs		medium	6–10 minutes
Fish			
large, whole	2.25–4.5 kg/5–10 lb	low/medium	allow 10 minutes per 0.5 cm/1 in thickness
small, whole	500–900 g/1¼–2 lb	medium/hot	12–20 minutes
sardines		medium/hot	4–6 minutes
fish steaks or fillets	2.5 cm/1 in	medium/hot	6–10 minutes
kebabs	2.5 cm/1 in	medium	5–8 minutes
large prawns, in shell		medium	6–8 minutes
large prawns, shelled		medium	4–6 minutes
scallops/mussels, in shell		medium	until open
scallops/mussels, shelled		medium	5–8 minutes
half lobster		low/medium	15–20 minutes

Barbecuing without meat

Cooking meat-free products on the barbecue can be quicker and safer than meat, as well as equally delicious and low in fat.

Cook kebabs made with vegetables for only a few minutes, remembering that these will need frequent turning and sprinkling with a little extra marinade to prevent them from burning. Kebabs made with tofu or paneer cubes will need only a little longer than this.

Potatoes on skewers will need to cook for longer. If cooked in foil, they will need up to an hour.

TECHNIQUES

Lighting the Fire

Follow these basic instructions when you light your fire, unless you have self-igniting charcoal, in which case you should follow the manufacturer's instructions carefully.

1 Spread a layer of foil over the base of the barbecue, to reflect the heat and to make cleaning easier.

2 It's a good idea to spread a layer of wood, charcoal or briquettes on the fire grate about 5 cm/2 in deep. Then you can pile the fuel in a small pyramid on top of this, in the centre.

3 Push one or two firelighter cubes into the centre of the pyramid or pour about 45ml/3 tbsp of liquid firelighter into the fuel and leave for 1 minute. Light with a long match or taper and leave to burn for 15 minutes. Spread the coals evenly and then leave for 30–45 minutes, until the coals are covered with a film of grey ash, before cooking.

Controlling the Heat

There are three basic ways to control the heat of the barbecue during cooking.

1 Raise or lower the height of the grill rack. Raise it for slow cooking, or use the bottom level for searing foods.

2 Push the burning coals apart for a lower heat; pile them closer together to increase the heat of the fire.

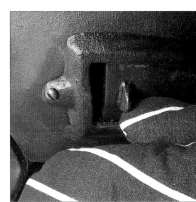

3 Most barbecues have air vents to allow air to the fire. Open them to make the fire hotter, or close them to lower the temperature.

COOK'S TIP
Try to find an area in the garden with a flat surface, where you can set up your barbecue.

Cooking in Foil Parcels

Delicate foods, or foods that are best cooked slowly in their own steam, can be cooked in foil parcels and either placed directly into the coals of the fire or on the barbecue rack. You can wrap all kinds of flavourings in the foil parcels, too.

1 Use heavy-duty cooking foil and cut two equal pieces, to make a double thickness, large enough to wrap the food. Lightly brush the centre of the foil with a little oil.

2 Place the food in the centre of the foil and add any flavourings and seasonings. Pull up the edges of the foil, on opposite sides, around the food.

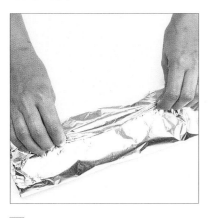

3 Make a double fold in the top of the foil to enclose the food in a parcel.

4 Fold over the ends, or twist them together, making sure the parcel is completely sealed, so that the juices cannot escape during cooking.

Preparing Whole Fish for Barbecuing

Small whole fish are ideal for barbecuing, especially oily fish such as mackerel or trout. Often they will already be prepared by the fishmonger, but if not they are very simple to prepare at home.

1 Cut off the fins and strip out the gills with scissors.

2 Hold the fish firmly at the tail end and use the back of a small knife blade or a special scaling tool to remove the scales, scraping towards the head end. Rinse under cold water.

3 Cut a long slit under the fish, from just under the tail to just behind the gills, to open up the belly. Use the knife to push out the entrails and discard them. Rinse the fish in cold water.

4 Rub the inside cavity of the fish with salt to clean it properly and rinse again; then dry with absorbent kitchen paper.

Barbecue Relish

Making use of storecupboard ingredients, this relish is ideal for use with kebabs, patties and other quick recipes.

INGREDIENTS
45 ml/3 tbsp sweet pickle
15 ml/1 tbsp Worcestershire sauce
30 ml/2 tbsp tomato ketchup
10 ml/2 tsp prepared mustard
15 ml/1 tbsp cider vinegar
30 ml/2 tbsp brown sauce

1 Place the sweet pickle in a medium-sized mixing bowl.

2 Stir in the Worcestershire sauce, tomato ketchup and prepared mustard.

3 Add the vinegar and brown sauce and mix well. Chill and use as required.

COOK'S TIP
This is a tangy, tasty relish, which is very easy to make.

Tomato Relish

This cooked relish may be served hot or cold. It has a concentrated tomato flavour, making it ideal with pasta, kebabs and barbecued meat.

INGREDIENTS
10 ml/2 tsp olive oil
1 onion, chopped
1 garlic clove, crushed
25 g/1 oz/2 tbsp flour
30 ml/2 tbsp tomato ketchup
300 ml/½ pint/1¼ cups passata
5 ml/1 tsp sugar
15 ml/1 tbsp chopped fresh parsley

1 Heat the oil in a pan. Add the onion and garlic clove and sauté for 5 minutes, stirring from time to time.

2 Stir in the flour and cook for a further minute.

3 Stir in the tomato ketchup, passata, sugar and fresh parsley. Bring to the boil. Chill and use as required.

COOK'S TIP
Passata is a smooth liquid made from sieved tomatoes. It is used as a base for recipes such as soups and sauces.

Chilli Relish

Not for the faint hearted, this warm relish is ideal served with snacks. If you prefer a slightly milder flavour, remove the seeds from the chilli before serving. Make sure that you wash your hands thoroughly after handling them.

INGREDIENTS
2 large tomatoes
1 red onion
10 ml/2 tsp chilli sauce
15 ml/1 tbsp chopped fresh basil
1 green chilli, chopped
pinch of salt
pinch of sugar

1 Finely chop the tomatoes and place in a mixing bowl.

2 Finely chop the onion and add to the tomatoes with the chilli sauce.

3 Stir in the fresh basil, chilli, salt and sugar. Use as required.

COOK'S TIP
Be as generous or as cautious as you like with the chilli, depending on how hot you like your food.

Cucumber Relish

A cool, refreshing relish, this may also be used as a dip, or as a sauce to serve with spicy chicken or kebabs. It should be used as quickly as possible – it is at its best when still very fresh, so that the cucumber pieces are still crunchy.

INGREDIENTS
½ cucumber
2 celery sticks, chopped
1 green pepper, seeded and chopped
1 garlic clove, crushed
300 ml/½ pint/1¼ cups plain low-fat
    natural yogurt
15 ml/1 tbsp chopped fresh coriander
freshly ground black pepper

1 Dice the cucumber and place in a large bowl.

2 Add the celery, green pepper and crushed garlic.

3 Stir in the yogurt and fresh coriander. Season with the pepper. Cover and chill.

COOK'S TIP
All these relishes should be used as quickly as possible, but will keep for up to a week in the fridge.

Mango and Radish Salsa

The sweet flavour and juicy texture of mango in this salsa is contrasted very well by the hot and crunchy radishes. Serve with pieces of barbecued fish or chicken.

VARIATION
Try using papaya in place of the mango in this salsa.

Serves 4

INGREDIENTS
1 large, ripe mango
12 radishes
juice of 1 lemon
15 ml/1 tbsp olive oil
red Tabasco sauce, to taste
45 ml/3 tbsp chopped fresh coriander
5 ml/1 tsp pink peppercorns
salt

mango

radishes

olive oil

lemon juice

fresh coriander

red Tabasco sauce

pink peppercorns

NUTRITIONAL NOTES
PER PORTION:

ENERGY 58 Kcals/242 KJ
FAT 2.9 g **SATURATED FAT** 0.5 g
CHOLESTEROL 0
FIBRE 2.0 g

1 Holding the mango upright on a chopping board, use a large knife to slice the flesh away from either side of the large flat stone in two pieces. Using a smaller knife, carefully trim away any flesh still clinging to the stone.

2 Score the flesh of the mango halves deeply, taking care to avoid cutting through the skin: make parallel incisions about 1 cm/½ in apart; turn and cut lines in the opposite direction. Carefully turn the skin inside out so the flesh stands out like hedgehog spikes. Slice the diced flesh away from the skin.

3 Trim the radishes, discarding the root tails and leaves. Coarsely grate the radishes or dice them finely and place in a bowl with the mango cubes.

4 Stir the lemon juice and olive oil with salt and a few drops of Tabasco sauce to taste, then stir in the chopped fresh coriander.

5 Coarsely crush the pink peppercorns with a pestle and mortar or place them on a chopping board and flatten them with the heel of a heavy-bladed knife. Stir into the lemon oil.

6 Gently mix together the radishes and mango, then pour in the dressing and toss again. Chill for up to 2 hours before serving.

Fiery Citrus Salsa

This unusual salsa makes a really fantastic marinade for fish and is also delicious drizzled over barbecued meat.

VARIATION

If you like things really fiery, don't seed the chillies! They will make the salsa particularly hot and fierce.

Serves 4

INGREDIENTS
1 orange
1 green apple
2 fresh red chillies
1 garlic clove
8 fresh mint leaves
juice of 1 lemon
salt and freshly ground black pepper
barbecued prawns, to serve

orange   *apple*

red chillies

garlic

lemon juice

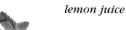

fresh mint

NUTRITIONAL NOTES
PER PORTION:

ENERGY 26 Kcals/111 KJ
FAT 0.1 g **SATURATED FAT** 0
CHOLESTEROL 0
FIBRE 1.1 g

1 Slice the bottom off the orange so that it will stand firmly on a chopping board. Using a sharp knife, remove the peel by slicing from the top to the bottom of the fruit.

2 Hold the orange in one hand over a bowl. Slice towards the middle of the fruit, to one side of a segment, and then gently twist the knife to ease the segment away from the membrane and out of the orange. Repeat to remove all the segments. Squeeze any juice from the remaining membrane into the bowl.

3 Peel the apple, making sure that it is peeled as thinly as possible. Then slice it neatly into wedges and carefully remove the core.

4 Halve the chillies and remove their seeds, then place them in a blender or food processor with the orange segments and juice, apple wedges, garlic and fresh mint.

5 Blend all the contents of the food processor until smooth. Then, with the motor still running, carefully pour in the lemon juice.

6 Season to taste with a little salt and pepper. Pour into a bowl or small jug and serve immediately with barbecued prawns or other kebabs.

Chunky Cherry Tomato Salsa

Succulent cherry tomatoes and refreshing cucumber form the basis of this delicious dill-seasoned salsa.

VARIATION
Try flavouring this salsa with other fragrant herbs, such as tarragon, coriander or even mint.

Serves 4

INGREDIENTS
1 ridge cucumber
5 ml/1 tsp sea salt
500 g/1¼ lb cherry tomatoes
1 garlic clove
1 lemon
15 ml/1 tbsp chilli oil
2.5 ml/½ tsp dried chilli flakes
30 ml/2 tbsp chopped fresh dill
salt and freshly ground black pepper

ridge cucumber

cherry tomatoes

chilli flakes

fresh dill

chilli oil

garlic

lemon

sea salt

NUTRITIONAL NOTES
PER PORTION:

ENERGY 53 Kcals/220 KJ
FAT 3.3 g **SATURATED FAT** 0.5 g
CHOLESTEROL 0
FIBRE 1.6 g

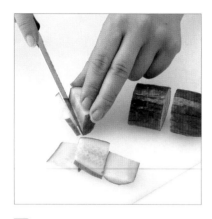

1 Trim the ends off the cucumber and cut it into 2.5 cm/1 in lengths, then cut each piece lengthways into thin slices.

2 Arrange the cucumber slices in a colander and sprinkle them with the sea salt. Leave for 5 minutes until the cucumber has wilted.

3 Wash the cucumber slices well under cold water and pat them dry with kitchen paper.

4 Quarter the cherry tomatoes and place in a bowl with the wilted cucumber. Finely chop the garlic.

5 Grate the lemon rind finely and place in a small jug with the juice from the lemon, the chilli oil, chilli flakes, dill and garlic. Add salt and pepper to taste, and whisk with a fork.

6 Pour the chilli oil dressing over the tomato and cucumber and toss well. Leave to marinate at room temperature for at least 2 hours before serving.

Saffron Dip

Serve this unusual and mild-flavoured dip with fresh vegetable crudités – it is particularly good with florets of cauliflower, asparagus tips and baby carrots and corn. Although saffron can be difficult to find, it is worth the trouble for this tasty dip.

Serves 4

INGREDIENTS
15 ml/1 tbsp boiling water
small pinch of saffron strands
200 g/7 oz/scant 1 cup fat-free
    fromage frais
10 fresh chives
10 fresh basil leaves
salt and freshly ground black pepper
vegetable crudités, to serve

saffron strands

fat-free fromage frais

fresh chives

fresh basil

NUTRITIONAL NOTES
PER PORTION:

ENERGY 30 Kcals/130 KJ
FAT 0.1 g SATURATED FAT 0.05 g
CHOLESTEROL 0.5 mg
FIBRE 0.05 g

1 Pour the boiling water into a bowl and add the saffron strands. Leave to infuse for 3 minutes.

2 Beat the fromage frais in a large bowl until smooth. Stir in the infused saffron liquid with a wooden spoon.

3 Snip the chives into the dip. Tear the basil leaves into small pieces and stir them in. Mix thoroughly.

4 Add salt and freshly ground black pepper to taste. Serve the dip with fresh vegetable crudités, if liked.

Potato Skins with Spicy Cajun Dip

As an alternative to deep-frying, barbecuing potato skins crisps them up in no time and gives them a wonderful char-grilled flavour. This spicy dip makes the perfect partner.

Serves 4

INGREDIENTS
4 large baking potatoes
15 ml/1 tbsp olive oil, for brushing
250 ml/8 fl oz/1 cup low-fat plain
    natural yogurt
2 garlic cloves, crushed
10 ml/2 tsp tomato purée
5 ml/1 tsp green chilli paste or 1
    small green chilli, chopped
2.5 ml/½ tsp celery salt
salt and freshly ground black pepper

baking
potatoes

low-fat
yogurt

tomato
purée

olive oil

garlic

green chilli
paste

celery salt

1 Prick the potatoes with a fork, then bake or microwave until tender. Cut them in half and scoop out the flesh, leaving a thin layer of potato on the skins. The scooped out potato can be reserved in the fridge or freezer for another meal.

2 Cut each potato shell in half again and lightly brush the skins with olive oil. Cook on a medium-hot barbecue for 4–5 minutes, or until crisp.

3 Mix together the remaining ingredients in a bowl to make the dip. Serve the potato skins with the Cajun dip on the side.

COOK'S TIP
If you don't have any chilli paste or fresh chillies, add one or two drops of hot pepper sauce to the dip instead. Make the dip hot or mild, according to taste.

NUTRITIONAL NOTES
PER PORTION:

ENERGY 293 Kcals/1250 KJ
FAT 2.1 g SATURATED FAT 0.5 g
CHOLESTEROL 2.5 mg
FIBRE 4.9 g

Guacamole with Crudités

This fresh-tasting spicy dip is made using peas instead of the traditional avocados for a light and fat-free version.

Serves 4

INGREDIENTS
350 g/12 oz/2¼ cups frozen
    peas, defrosted
1 garlic clove, crushed
2 spring onions, trimmed
    and chopped
5 ml/1 tsp finely grated rind and juice
    of 1 lime, plus extra juice to serve
2.5 ml/½ tsp ground cumin
dash of Tabasco sauce
15 ml/1 tbsp reduced-calorie
    mayonnaise
30 ml/2 tbsp chopped fresh coriander
salt and freshly ground black pepper
pinch of paprika and lime slices,
    to garnish
baby carrots, celery sticks, eating
    apples, pears and baby sweetcorn,
    to serve

peas

spring onions

garlic

ground cumin

Tabasco sauce

fresh corriander

reduced-calorie mayonnaise

lime

1 Mix the peas, garlic clove, spring onions, lime rind and juice, cumin, Tabasco sauce, mayonnaise and salt and pepper in a food processor or a blender for a few minutes until smooth.

2 Add the chopped coriander and process for a few more seconds. Spoon into a serving bowl, cover with clear film and chill in the fridge for about 30 minutes, to let the flavours develop.

3 Prepare the fruit and vegetables for the crudités. Trim and peel the carrots. Halve the celery sticks lengthways and trim into sticks, the same length as the carrots. Quarter, core and thickly slice the apples and pears, then dip into the extra lime juice. Arrange all the prepared crudités with the baby sweetcorn on a platter to serve with the guacamole.

4 Sprinkle the paprika over the guacamole and garnish with lime slices.

NUTRITIONAL NOTES
PER PORTION:

ENERGY 112 Kcals/473 KJ
FAT 1.9 g **SATURATED FAT** 0.2 g
CHOLESTEROL 0
FIBRE 6.7 g

Tsatziki

You can serve this classic Greek dip with strips of pitta bread toasted on the barbecue. The tangy cucumber makes it a light, refreshing snack.

Serves 4

INGREDIENTS
1 mini cucumber
4 spring onions
1 garlic clove
200 ml/7 fl oz/scant 1 cup low-fat
    Greek-style yogurt
45ml/3 tbsp chopped fresh mint
salt and freshly ground black pepper
fresh mint sprig, to garnish (optional)
toasted pitta bread, to serve

mini cucumber   *garlic*

spring onions

low-fat Greek-style yogurt

fresh mint

1 Trim the ends from the cucumber, then cut it into 5 mm/¼ in dice.

2 Trim the spring onions and garlic, then chop both very finely.

3 Beat the yogurt until smooth, if necessary, then gently stir in the cucumber, onions, garlic and mint.

4 Transfer the mixture to a serving bowl and add salt and plenty of freshly ground black pepper to taste. Chill until ready to serve and then garnish with a small mint sprig, if liked. Serve with slices of pitta bread that has been toasted on the barbecue, if you like.

NUTRITIONAL NOTES
PER PORTION:

ENERGY 34 Kcals/143 KJ
FAT 0.5 g SATURATED FAT 0.25 g
CHOLESTEROL 2 mg
FIBRE 0.4 g

COOK'S TIP

Choose Greek-style low-fat yogurt for this dip – it has a delicious creamy texture without the fat of regular Greek-style yogurt. You can find it in most large supermarkets.

Chicken and Pineapple Kebabs

NUTRITIONAL NOTES
Per portion:

ENERGY 94.8 Kcals/400 KJ
FAT 2.2 g **SATURATED FAT** 0.6 g
CHOLESTEROL 19.8 mg
FIBRE 1.2 g

This chicken has a delicate tang and is very tender. The pineapple gives a slight sweetness to the chicken and keeps it succulent during cooking.

Serves 6

INGREDIENTS
225 g/8 oz can pineapple chunks in
    natural juice
5 ml/1 tsp ground cumin
5 ml/1 tsp ground coriander
1 small garlic clove, crushed
5 ml/1 tsp chilli powder
5 ml/1 tsp salt
30 ml/2 tbsp low-fat natural yogurt
15 ml/1 tbsp chopped fresh coriander
few drops of orange food
    colouring (optional)
275 g/10 oz skinless, boneless
    chicken breasts
½ red pepper
½ yellow or green pepper
1 large onion
9 cherry tomatoes
10 ml/2 tsp corn oil
salad or boiled rice, to serve

chicken breasts

ground coriander

peppers   *salt*

ground cumin

low-fat yogurt

onion

chilli powder

fresh coriander

cherry tomatoes

garlic

pineapple

corn oil

1 Drain the pineapple juice into a bowl. Reserve 12 large chunks of pineapple and squeeze the juice from the remaining chunks into the bowl and set aside. You should have 120 ml/ 4 fl oz/½ cup of pineapple juice. Make up with water if necessary.

2 In a large mixing bowl, combine the ground cumin, ground coriander, garlic, chilli powder, salt, yogurt, fresh coriander and food colouring, if using. Pour in the reserved pineapple juice and mix well.

3 Cut the chicken into bite-size cubes, add to the yogurt and spice mixture, cover and leave to marinate for about 1–1½ hours in a cool place. Meanwhile cut the peppers and onion into bite-size chunks.

4 Drain the chicken pieces, reserving the marinade, and thread on to six wooden or metal skewers, alternating with the vegetables, cherry tomatoes and reserved pineapple chunks.

5 Brush the kebabs with the oil, then grill on a medium-hot barbecue, turning and basting the chicken pieces with the marinade regularly, for 15 minutes, or until the chicken is cooked. Serve with salad or plain boiled rice.

Citrus Kebabs

Serve these succulent barbecued chicken kebabs on a bed of lettuce leaves, garnished with sprigs of fresh mint and orange and lemon slices.

Serves 4

INGREDIENTS
4 skinless, boneless chicken breasts
fresh mint sprigs, to garnish
orange, lemon or lime slices,
   to garnish

FOR THE MARINADE
finely grated rind and juice of
   ¹/₂ orange
finely grated rind and juice of
   ¹/₂ lemon or lime
10 ml/2 tsp olive oil
30 ml/2 tbsp clear honey
30 ml/2 tbsp chopped fresh mint
1.5 ml/¹/₄ tsp ground cumin
salt and freshly ground black pepper

1 Use a sharp knife to cut the chicken into 2.5 cm/1 in cubes.

chicken breasts   *orange*   *lemon*

olive oil   *clear honey*   *fresh mint*   *ground cumin*

VARIATION
You can vary the citrus juices if you like – including grapefruit, perhaps, which has a slightly bitter flavour. Garnish the dish with sprigs of fresh coriander instead of mint.

2 Mix together the marinade ingredients in a large bowl, add the chicken and cover with clear film. Leave to marinate for at least 2 hours in a cool place, or overnight in the fridge.

3 Thread the chicken on to metal skewers and cook on a medium barbecue for 10 minutes, basting with the marinade and turning frequently. Garnish with mint and citrus slices.

Caribbean Chicken Kebabs

These kebabs have a rich, robust flavour and the marinade keeps them moist without the need for oil. Serve with a salad or in pitta bread pockets.

Serves 4

INGREDIENTS
500 g/1¼ lb skinless, boneless
    chicken breasts
finely grated rind of 1 lime
30 ml/2 tbsp fresh lime juice
15 ml/1 tbsp rum or sherry
15 ml/1 tbsp light muscovado sugar
5 ml/1 tsp ground cinnamon
2 mangoes, peeled and cubed
rice and salad, to serve

chicken breasts

lime

rum   *mangoes*

*light
muscovado
sugar*   *ground
cinnamon*

NUTRITIONAL NOTES
PER PORTION:

ENERGY 190 Kcals/803 KJ
FAT 4.1 g SATURATED FAT 1.3 g
CHOLESTEROL 53.8 mg
FIBRE 1.8 g

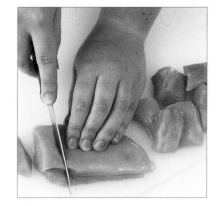

1 Cut the chicken into bite-size chunks and place in a bowl with the lime rind and juice, rum or sherry, sugar and cinnamon. Toss well, cover and leave to stand for 1 hour in a cool place.

2 Cut the mangoes into cubes by cutting slices, scoring into cubes and slicing away from the skin.

COOK'S TIP
Soak the skewers in cold water for 30 minutes before filling them. This prevents the wood from scorching.

3 Drain the chicken, saving the juices and thread on to four wooden skewers, alternating with the mango cubes.

4 Grill the skewers on a hot barbecue for 8–10 minutes, turning occasionally and basting with the juices, until the chicken is tender and golden brown. Serve at once with rice and a salad of your choice, if you like.

Mediterranean Skewers

Barbecuing intensifies the delicious Mediterranean flavours of the vegetables in this recipe.

Serves 4

INGREDIENTS
2 medium courgettes
1 long thin aubergine
300 g/11 oz boneless turkey, cut into
    5 cm/2 in cubes
12–16 pickling onions or 4 medium
    onions, halved
1 red or yellow pepper, cut into
    5 cm/2 in squares

FOR THE MARINADE
45 ml/3 tbsp olive oil
45 ml/3 tbsp fresh lemon juice
1 garlic clove, finely chopped
30 ml/2 tbsp chopped fresh basil
salt and freshly ground black pepper

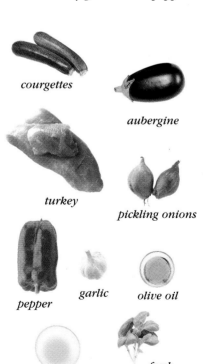

courgettes

aubergine

turkey

pickling onions

pepper   garlic   olive oil

lemon juice   fresh basil

1 Mix the marinade ingredients together in a bowl and leave aside.

2 Slice the courgettes and aubergine lengthways into strips 5 mm/¼ in thick. Cut them crossways about two-thirds down their length. Discard the shorter lengths. Wrap half the turkey with courgette slices and half with aubergine.

NUTRITIONAL NOTES
PER PORTION:

ENERGY 134 Kcals/565 KJ
FAT 4.6 g SATURATED FAT 0.9 g
CHOLESTEROL 45.8 mg
FIBRE 1.9 g

3 Prepare the skewers by alternating the turkey, onions and pepper pieces. Sprinkle with the flavoured oil. Leave to marinate for at least 30 minutes.

4 Cook on a medium-hot barbecue, turning the skewers occasionally, for 10 minutes, or until the turkey is cooked and the vegetables are tender. Serve.

Tandoori Chicken Kebabs

This dish originates from the plains of the Punjab at the foot of the Himalayas, where food is traditionally cooked in clay ovens known as tandoors – hence the name.

Serves 4

INGREDIENTS

4 skinless, boneless chicken breasts
(about 90 g/3½ oz each)
15 ml/1 tbsp lemon juice
45ml/3 tbsp tandoori paste
45ml/3 tbsp low-fat natural yogurt
1 garlic clove, crushed
30 ml/2 tbsp chopped fresh coriander
1 small onion, cut into wedges and
separated into layers
salt and freshly ground black pepper
fresh coriander sprigs, to garnish
pilau rice and naan bread, to serve

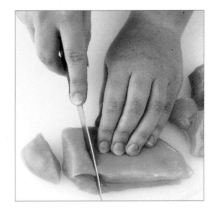

1 Chop the chicken breasts into 2.5 cm/1 in cubes and place in a bowl.

chicken breasts

lemon juice

tandoori paste

fresh coriander

onion

garlic

low-fat yogurt

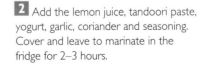

COOK'S TIP
Use strips of skinless, boneless turkey breasts, for a cheaper and equally low fat alternative. Remember to serve with a fat-free salad for a particularly healthy meal.

NUTRITIONAL NOTES

PER PORTION:

ENERGY 166 Kcals/700 KJ
FAT 5 g SATURATED FAT 1.4 g
CHOLESTEROL 56.3 mg
FIBRE 0

2 Add the lemon juice, tandoori paste, yogurt, garlic, coriander and seasoning. Cover and leave to marinate in the fridge for 2–3 hours.

3 Thread alternate pieces of chicken and onion on to four skewers. Cook them over a hot barbecue for about 10–12 minutes, turning once. Make sure that the onions do not burn. Garnish with coriander sprigs and serve at once with pilau rice and naan bread, if liked.

Sweet and Sour Kebabs

This marinade contains sugar and will burn very easily, so cook the kebabs slowly and turn them often. Serve with a fat-free salad of your choice.

Serves 4

INGREDIENTS
2 skinless, boneless chicken breasts
8 pickling onions or 2
    medium onions
3 firm bananas
4 lean back bacon rashers
1 red pepper, diced
sprigs of fresh parsley, to garnish
rice or salad, to serve

FOR THE MARINADE
30 ml/2 tbsp soft brown sugar
15 ml/1 tbsp Worcestershire sauce
30 ml/2 tbsp lemon juice
salt and freshly ground black pepper

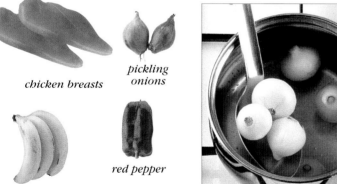

chicken breasts   *pickling onions*

bananas   *red pepper*

soft brown sugar   *Worcestershire sauce*

bacon   *lemon juice*

1 Mix together the marinade ingredients. Cut each chicken breast into four, add the marinade, cover and leave for at least 4 hours in the fridge.

2 Peel the onions, blanch them in boiling water for 5 minutes and drain. Quarter them if using medium onions.

NUTRITIONAL NOTES
PER PORTION:

ENERGY 304 Kcals/1288 KJ
FAT 5 g **SATURATED FAT** 1.6 g
CHOLESTEROL 30.5 mg
FIBRE 3.4 g

3 Peel all the bananas and cut each one into three or four pieces, depending on the size of the bananas, to make nine or 12 pieces in all. Cut the bacon rashers into the same number of pieces and wrap one piece around each banana slice.

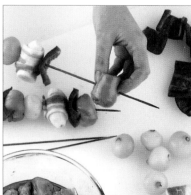

4 Thread the bananas on to skewers with the chicken pieces, onions and pepper pieces. Brush generously with the marinade. Cook on a low barbecue for 15 minutes, turning frequently and basting when necessary. Serve with rice or salad, and garnish with parsley sprigs.

Turkey Sosaties with a Curried Apricot Sauce

This is a South African way of cooking meat or poultry in a delicious sweet and sour sauce spiced with curry powder.

Serves 4

INGREDIENTS

5 ml/1 tsp vegetable oil
1 onion, finely chopped
1 garlic clove, crushed
2 bay leaves
juice of 1 lemon
30 ml/2 tbsp curry powder
60 ml/4 tbsp apricot jam
60 ml/4 tbsp apple juice
675 g/1½ lb turkey fillet
30 ml/2 tbsp low-fat crème fraîche
salt

onion

garlic

apple juice

bay leaves

curry powder

lemon juice

vegetable oil

turkey

apricot jam

low-fat crème fraîche

1 Heat the oil in a saucepan. Add the onion, garlic and bay leaves and cook over a low heat for 10 minutes until the onions are soft. Add the lemon juice, curry powder, apricot jam and apple juice, with salt to taste. Cook gently for 5 minutes. Leave to cool.

2 Cut the turkey into evenly sized cubes about 2 cm/¾ in thick.

3 Add to the apricot marinade. Mix well, cover and leave in a cool place to marinate for at least 2 hours or overnight in the fridge. Thread the turkey on to skewers, allowing the marinade to run back into the bowl. Grill the sosaties over a medium-hot barbecue for 6–8 minutes, turning several times, until cooked.

4 Meanwhile, transfer the reserved apricot marinade to a pan and simmer gently over a low heat for about 2 minutes. Then stir in the crème fraîche and serve immediately with the hot turkey sosaties.

NUTRITIONAL NOTES

PER PORTION:

ENERGY 200 Kcals/845 KJ
FAT 2.8 g **SATURATED FAT** 0.7 g
CHOLESTEROL 83 mg
FIBRE 0.8 g

Chicken Pittas with Red Coleslaw

Pittas are convenient for simple snacks and picnics and it's easy to pack in plenty of fresh, healthy ingredients. This recipe is ideal for pieces of chicken breast that have already been barbecued.

Serves 4

INGREDIENTS
¼ red cabbage
1 small red onion, finely sliced
2 radishes, thinly sliced
1 red apple, peeled, cored and grated
15 ml/1 tbsp lemon juice
45 ml/3 tbsp fat-free fromage frais
1 cooked skinless, boneless chicken
   breast, about 175 g/6 oz
4 large or 8 small pitta breads
salt and freshly ground black pepper
chopped fresh parsley, to garnish

red cabbage *red onion*

lemon juice
red apple *radishes*

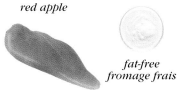
fat-free fromage frais *pitta breads*
chicken breast

NUTRITIONAL NOTES
PER PORTION:

ENERGY 293 Kcals/1250 KJ
FAT 2.8 g **SATURATED FAT** 0.5 g
CHOLESTEROL 24.5 mg
FIBRE 5.5 g

1 Remove the tough central stalk from the cabbage, then finely shred the leaves using a large sharp knife. Place the shredded cabbage in a bowl. Stir in the onion, radishes, apple and lemon juice.

COOK'S TIP
Use freshly cooked pieces of chicken, straight from the barbecue, removing any bones. You can also use any cold leftover pieces from a barbecue party the day before, as long as the pieces have been refrigerated.

2 Stir the fromage frais into the cabbage mixture and season well. Finely slice the cooked chicken breast and stir into the cabbage mixture until well coated in fromage frais.

3 Toast the pittas on a barbecue over a low heat, then split them along one edge using a round-bladed knife. Spoon the filling into the pittas, then garnish with the chopped fresh parsley.

Bacon Koftas

These koftas are easy to make and are good served with rice and lots of salad. Although bacon can be high in fat in itself, it is used more as a flavouring in this recipe – a very effective way of livening up low-fat barbecue food.

Serves 4

INGREDIENTS
175 g/6 oz lean bacon
250 ml/1 cup fresh wholemeal
    breadcrumbs
2 spring onions, chopped
15 ml/1 tbsp chopped fresh parsley
finely grated rind of 1 lemon
1 egg white
freshly ground black pepper
paprika, for sprinkling
lemon rind and fresh parsley leaves,
    to garnish
rice and salad, to serve

fresh parsley

spring onions

lemon   *egg white*   *bacon*

breadcrumbs   *paprika*

1 Remove any pieces of fat that may be on the bacon slices and cut them coarsely. Place the bacon in a food processor together with the breadcrumbs, spring onions, parsley, lemon rind, egg white and pepper. Process the mixture until it is finely chopped and begins to bind together.

NUTRITIONAL NOTES
PER PORTION:

ENERGY 289 Kcals/1229 KJ
FAT 4.4 g **SATURATED FAT** 1.1 g
CHOLESTEROL 7.5 mg
FIBRE 1.6 g

VARIATION
You can add virtually anything you like to give flavour to these simple koftas. Use chopped fresh mint or basil instead of the parsley, and a lime instead of the lemon.

2 Divide the bacon mixture into eight pieces and mould into long oval shapes, wrapped around eight wooden or bamboo skewers.

3 Sprinkle the koftas with paprika and cook on a hot barbecue for 8–10 minutes, turning occasionally, until browned and cooked through. Garnish with lemon rind and parsley leaves, then serve hot with rice and a salad.

COOK'S TIP
Remember to soak the wooden or bamboo skewers before wrapping the bacon koftas around them. This should prevent them burning over the barbecue.

Chicken with Lime

Limes can be used in the same way as lemons but provide more of a colour contrast – particularly when mixed with fresh coriander.

Serves 4

INGREDIENTS
4 skinless, boneless chicken breasts
2 limes and 4-6 coriander sprigs,
    to garnish

FOR THE MARINADE
1 small onion, finely chopped
15 ml/1 tbsp finely grated or crushed
    fresh root ginger
15 ml/1 tbsp crushed garlic
30 ml/2 tbsp dark soy sauce
10 ml/2 tsp ground coriander
5 ml/1 tsp ground cumin
15 ml/1 tbsp dark brown sugar
15 ml/1 tbsp sunflower oil

root ginger

chicken breasts

dark brown sugar

onion

ground coriander

garlic

sunflower oil

ground cumin

soy sauce

1 Cut the chicken breasts into strips and mix with the marinade ingredients. Cover and leave in the fridge for 4 hours.

2 Using a cannelle knife, cut decorative strips lengthwise down the skin of one of the limes at 1 cm/½ in intervals, then cut the lime into slices about 5 mm/¼ in thick. Make a cut from the centre of each slice to the edge and twist to an "S" shape. Cut the remaining lime in half lengthwise and place cut-side down. Make three V-shaped cuts into each of the lime halves, one below the other, and push each wedge out slightly to give a stepped effect.

3 Drain the chicken strips, reserving the marinade for later use. Thread on to wooden skewers.

4 Cook on a barbecue over moderately hot coals for about 15 minutes, or until tender, turning frequently and brushing occasionally with the reserved marinade to keep the meat moist. Serve garnished with the limes and coriander sprigs.

NUTRITIONAL NOTES
PER PORTION:

ENERGY 161 Kcals/680 KJ
FAT 4.8 g SATURATED FAT 1.3 g
CHOLESTEROL 53.7 mg
FIBRE 0.2 g

Chicken Tikka

The red food colouring gives this dish its traditional bright colour. Serve with lemon wedges and a crisp mixed salad.

Serves 4

INGREDIENTS
4 skinless chicken breasts
lemon wedges and mixed salad
    leaves, e.g. frisée and oakleaf
    lettuce or radicchio, to serve

FOR THE MARINADE
150 ml/¼ pint/⅔ cup plain low-fat
    natural yogurt
5 ml/1 tsp paprika
10 ml/2 tsp grated fresh root ginger
1 garlic clove, crushed
10 ml/2 tsp garam masala
2.5 ml/½ tsp salt
few drops of red food
    colouring (optional)
juice of 1 lemon

1 Mix all the marinade ingredients in a large dish. Add the chicken pieces to coat for at least 4 hours or overnight in the fridge, to allow the flavours to penetrate the flesh.

lemon juice

chicken breasts

paprika

ginger

garam masala

low-fat yogurt

garlic

salt

COOK'S TIP
This is an example of a dish that is usually very high in fat, but with a few basic changes this level can be dramatically reduced. This can also be achieved in other similar dishes, by substituting low-fat yogurt for full-fat versions and creams, by removing skin from chicken, as well as by reducing the amount of oil.

NUTRITIONAL NOTES
PER PORTION:

ENERGY 160 Kcals/676 KJ
FAT 4.3 g SATURATED FAT 1.4 g
CHOLESTEROL 54.5 mg
FIBRE 0.4 g

2 Remove the chicken pieces from the marinade and cook over a hot barbecue for 30–40 minutes or until tender, turning occasionally and basting with a little of the marinade.

3 Arrange on a bed of salad leaves with two lemon wedges and serve either hot or cold.

Chicken in Spicy Yogurt

Plan this dish well in advance as the chicken needs to marinate for a while to develop a spicy flavour.

NUTRITIONAL NOTES
PER PORTION:

ENERGY 126 Kcals/532 KJ
FAT 3.2 g SATURATED FAT 1 g
CHOLESTEROL 43 mg
FIBRE 0.1 g

Serves 6

INGREDIENTS
6 chicken pieces
juice of 1 lemon
5 ml/1 tsp salt
lemon or lime wedges and lettuce
    leaves, to garnish

FOR THE MARINADE
5 ml/1 tsp coriander seeds
10 ml/2 tsp cumin seeds
6 cloves
2 bay leaves
1 onion, quartered
2 garlic cloves
5 cm/2 in piece fresh root ginger,
    peeled and roughly chopped
2.5 ml/¹/₂ tsp chilli powder
5 ml/1 tsp turmeric
150 ml/¹/₄ pint/²/₃ cup plain low-fat
    natural yogurt

chicken pieces
lemon juice
low-fat yogurt
root ginger
onion
salt
garlic
coriander seeds
cloves
bay leaves
cumin seeds
chilli powder
turmeric

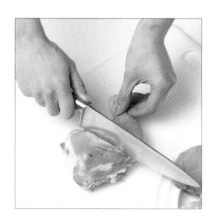

1 Skin the chicken joints and make deep slashes in the fleshiest parts with a sharp knife. Sprinkle over the lemon juice and salt and rub in.

2 Spread the coriander and cumin seeds, cloves and bay leaves in the bottom of a large frying pan and dry-fry over a moderate heat until the bay leaves are crispy.

3 Cool the spices and grind coarsely with a pestle and mortar.

4 Finely mince the onion, garlic and ginger in a food processor or blender. Add the ground spices, chilli, turmeric and yogurt, then strain in the lemon juice from the chicken.

5 Arrange the chicken in a single layer in a shallow dish. Pour over the marinade, then cover and chill for about 24–36 hours, occasionally turning the chicken pieces in the marinade.

6 Remove the chicken pieces and cook over a low barbecue for about 30–45 minutes, turning the pieces and basting with the marinade occasionally. Serve hot or cold, garnished with fresh leaves and wedges of lemon or lime.

Grilled Fish in Banana Leaves

Fish prepared in this way is particularly succulent and flavoursome as well as being easy to barbecue. Fillets are used here rather than whole fish, which makes it easier for those who don't like to mess about with bones.

Serves 4

INGREDIENTS

175 g/6 oz mixed vegetables, such as carrots or leeks
250 ml/8 fl oz/1 cup coconut milk
30 ml/2 tbsp red curry paste
45 ml/3 tbsp fish sauce
30 ml/2 tbsp caster sugar
5 kaffir lime leaves, torn
4 x 175 g/6 oz fish fillets, such as snapper
4 banana leaves or pieces of foil
30 ml/2 tbsp shredded spring onions, to garnish
2 red chillies, finely sliced, to garnish

coconut milk

red curry paste

fish sauce

caster sugar

lime leaves

fish fillets

banana leaves

mixed vegetables

1 Prepare the vegetables. Wash and peel them as necessary and shred finely. Meanwhile, combine the coconut milk, curry paste, fish sauce, sugar and kaffir lime leaves in a dish. Marinate the fish in the mixture for 15–30 minutes.

2 Mix together the vegetables and lay a portion on top of a banana leaf or piece of foil. Place a piece of fish on top with a little of its marinade.

3 Wrap up the fish in a leaf parcel and secure with cocktail sticks. (With foil, just crumple the edges together.) Repeat with the rest of the fish.

4 Cook on a medium-hot barbecue for 20–25 minutes or until the fish is cooked. Just before serving, garnish the fish with a sprinkling of spring onions and sliced red chillies.

NUTRITIONAL NOTES

PER PORTION:

ENERGY 289 Kcals/1229 KJ
FAT 4.4 g **SATURATED FAT** 0.9 g
CHOLESTEROL 147 mg
FIBRE 1.2 g

Tuna and Corn Fish Cakes

These little tuna fish cakes are quick both to make and to cook on the barbecue. Use fresh mashed potatoes or instant, if short of time.

Serves 4

INGREDIENTS

350 ml/1½ cups cooked,
    mashed potatoes
200 g/7 oz can tuna in brine, drained
175 ml/¾ cup canned or
    frozen sweetcorn
30 ml/2 tbsp chopped fresh parsley
250 ml/1 cup fresh white or
    wholemeal breadcrumbs
salt and freshly ground black pepper
lemon wedges and fresh vegetables,
    to serve (optional)

mashed potatoes

tuna

sweetcorn

fresh parsley

breadcrumbs

NUTRITIONAL NOTES

PER PORTION:

ENERGY 387 Kcals/1645 KJ
FAT 2.7 g SATURATED FAT 0.2 g
CHOLESTEROL 25 mg
FIBRE 2.2 g

1 Place the mashed potato in a bowl and stir in the tuna, sweetcorn and chopped parsley.

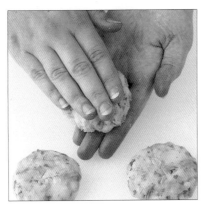

2 Season to taste with salt and pepper, then shape into eight fish cakes with your hands.

VARIATION

For simple variations that are just as good, try using canned sardines, red or pink salmon or smoked mackerel in place of the tuna.

3 Spread out the breadcrumbs on a plate and press the fish cakes into the crumbs to coat lightly.

4 Cook the fish cakes over a moderately hot barbecue until crisp and golden brown, turning once. Take care that they do not break up. Serve at once, with lemon wedges and fresh vegetables, if you like.

Halibut with Fresh Tomato and Basil Salsa

Try using a fish rack for this dish, as halibut breaks easily when the skin has been removed.

Serves 4

INGREDIENTS
4 halibut fillets, about 150 g/
   5 oz each
10 ml/2 tsp olive oil

FOR THE SALSA
1 medium tomato, roughly chopped
¼ red onion, finely chopped
1 small jalapeño pepper
30 ml/2 tbsp balsamic vinegar
10 large fresh basil leaves
5 ml/1 tsp olive oil
salt and freshly ground black pepper

halibut fillets

tomato

jalapeño pepper

balsamic vinegar

red onion

olive oil

basil leaves

NUTRITIONAL NOTES
PER PORTION:

ENERGY 202 Kcals/857 KJ
FAT 5 g **SATURATED FAT** 0.9 g
CHOLESTEROL 61.5 mg
FIBRE 0.25 g

1 To make the salsa, mix together the chopped tomato, red onion, jalapeño pepper and balsamic vinegar in a bowl.

2 Slice the fresh basil leaves finely, using a sharp kitchen knife.

VARIATION
Use any other white fish that you have to hand, such as cod, sole or whiting – it will be just as good.

3 Stir the basil and the olive oil into the tomato mixture. Season to taste. Cover the bowl with clear film and leave to marinate for at least 3 hours.

4 Brush the halibut fillets with oil and season. Cook on a medium barbecue for 8 minutes, and turning once. Serve with the salsa.

Swordfish Kebabs

Swordfish has a firm meaty texture that makes it ideal for cooking on a barbecue. Marinate the fish first to keep it moist.

Serves 6

INGREDIENTS
675 g/1½ lb swordfish steaks
15 ml/1 tbsp olive oil
juice of 1 lemon
1 garlic clove, crushed
5 ml/1 tsp paprika
2 onions
3 tomatoes
salt and freshly ground black pepper
salad and pitta bread, to serve

swordfish steaks

olive oil

lemon juice

garlic

paprika

tomatoes

onions

1 Use a large kitchen knife to cut the swordfish steaks into large cubes. Arrange the cubes in a single layer in a large shallow dish. Blend together the olive oil, lemon juice, garlic, paprika and seasoning in a bowl, and pour this over the fish. Cover the dish loosely with clear film and leave to marinate in a cool place for up to 2 hours.

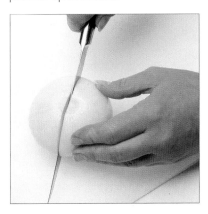

2 Peel the onions and cut them into large wedges.

3 Cut each tomato in half and then cut again into quarters.

4 Thread the fish cubes on to metal skewers, alternating them with the pieces of tomato and onion wedges. Cook the kebabs on a hot barbecue for 5–10 minutes, basting frequently with the remaining marinade and turning occasionally. Serve with salad and warm pitta bread.

Grilled Snapper with Hot Mango Salsa

A ripe mango provides the basis for a deliciously rich fruity salsa. The dressing needs no oil and features the tropical flavours of coriander, ginger and chilli.

Serves 4

INGREDIENTS

4 red snapper, about 250 g/9 oz each, cleaned, scaled and gutted
10 ml/2 tsp olive oil
salt and freshly ground black pepper
lettuce leaves, mixed vegetables, cherry tomatoes and hard-boiled eggs, to serve (optional)

FOR THE SALSA

45ml/3 tbsp chopped fresh coriander
1 medium ripe mango, peeled, stoned and diced
1/2 red chilli, seeded and chopped
2.5 cm/1 in fresh root ginger, grated
juice of 2 limes
generous pinch of celery salt

1 Using a sharp knife, slash each snapper three times on either side. Brush with the olive oil and cook on a medium-hot barbecue for 12 minutes, turning once.

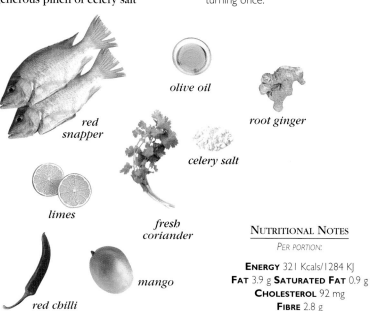

red snapper

olive oil

root ginger

celery salt

limes

fresh coriander

NUTRITIONAL NOTES

PER PORTION:

ENERGY 321 Kcals/1284 KJ
FAT 3.9 g SATURATED FAT 0.9 g
CHOLESTEROL 92 mg
FIBRE 2.8 g

mango

red chilli

2 To make the salsa, place the chopped fresh coriander in a food processor. Add the mango chunks, chilli, grated ginger, lime juice and celery salt and process until smooth.

3 Distribute the lettuce leaves evenly between four large plates.

4 Arrange the snapper on the lettuce and season to taste. Serve immediately with mixed vegetables, cherry tomatoes and hard-boiled eggs, if you like, or substitute for a fat-free salad. Accompany the meal with the salsa.

VARIATION

If fresh mangoes are unavailable, use canned ones, draining well. Sea bream can also be used for this recipe, if you prefer.

Calamari with Two-tomato Stuffing

Calamari, or baby squid, are quick to cook, but make sure that you turn and baste them often. Don't overcook them or they will toughen.

Serves 4

INGREDIENTS
500 g/1¼ lb baby squid, cleaned
1 garlic clove, crushed
3 plum tomatoes, skinned
    and chopped
8 sun-dried tomatoes, chopped
60 ml/4 tbsp chopped fresh basil,
    plus extra, to serve
60 ml/4 tbsp fresh white
    breadcrumbs
15 ml/1 tbsp olive oil, plus extra
    for brushing
15 ml/1 tbsp red wine vinegar
salt and freshly ground black pepper
lemon wedges and juice, to serve

baby squid

breadcrumbs

garlic

plum tomatoes

fresh basil

sun-dried tomatoes

olive oil   *red wine vinegar*

1 Remove the tentacles from the squid and roughly chop them; leave the main part of the squid whole.

2 Mix together the garlic, plum tomatoes, sun-dried tomatoes, basil and breadcrumbs, and stir well. Then stir in the olive oil and the red wine vinegar. Season well with plenty of salt and pepper. Soak some wooden cocktail sticks in water for at least 10 minutes before use, to prevent them from burning.

3 With a teaspoon, fill the squid with the stuffing mixture. Secure the open ends with the cocktail sticks.

4 Brush the squid with a little olive oil and cook over a medium-hot barbecue for 4–5 minutes, turning often. Sprinkle with lemon juice and extra basil to serve, with lemon wedges on the side.

COOK'S TIP
You can often buy ready-prepared squid in packets from good supermarkets, which will save you a lot of time.

NUTRITIONAL NOTES
PER PORTION:

ENERGY 183 Kcals/779 KJ
FAT 4.6 g SATURATED FAT 0.8 g
CHOLESTEROL 281 mg
FIBRE 0.7 g

Cajun-style Cod

This recipe works equally well with any firm-fleshed fish such as swordfish, shark, tuna or halibut. The herbs and spices here create a wonderful, pungent aroma and a taste that will make your mouth water.

Serves 4

INGREDIENTS
4 cod steaks, each weighing about
    175 g/6 oz
30 ml/2 tbsp low-fat natural yogurt
15 ml/1 tbsp lime or lemon juice
1 garlic clove, crushed
5 ml/1 tsp ground cumin
5 ml/1 tsp paprika
5 ml/1 tsp mustard powder
2.5 ml/½ tsp cayenne pepper
2.5 ml/½ tsp dried thyme
2.5 ml/½ tsp dried oregano
new potatoes and a mixed salad,
    to serve (optional)

low-fat yogurt

garlic

cayenne pepper

ground cumin

lime

cod

dried thyme

mustard powder

paprika

dried oregano

1 Pat the fish dry with absorbent kitchen paper. Mix together the yogurt and lime or lemon juice and brush lightly over both sides of the fish.

2 Mix together the crushed garlic, spices and herbs. Coat both sides of the fish with the seasoning mix, making sure that it is well rubbed in.

3 Cook the fish over a hot barbecue for 4 minutes, or until the underside is well browned.

4 Turn over and cook for a further 4 minutes, or until the steaks have cooked through. Serve immediately, with new potatoes and a mixed salad, if liked.

NUTRITIONAL NOTES
PER PORTION:

ENERGY 172 Kcals/732 KJ
FAT 2.2 g SATURATED FAT 0.5 g
CHOLESTEROL 98 mg
FIBRE 0

COOK'S TIP
Using a fish rack, or placing a smaller grill pan rack on your barbecue grid, will make it easier to cook fish without it breaking up.

Spiced Prawns with Vegetables

This is a light and nutritious Indian dish, excellent served either on a bed of lettuce or with rice.

Serves 4

INGREDIENTS
20 cooked king prawns, peeled
1 medium courgette, thickly sliced
1 medium onion, cut into 8 chunks
8 cherry tomatoes
8 baby sweetcorn
mixed salad leaves, to serve

FOR THE MARINADE
30 ml/2 tbsp chopped fresh coriander
5 ml/1 tsp salt
2 fresh green chillies, seeded
    if wished
45 ml/3 tbsp lemon juice
10 ml/2 tsp olive oil

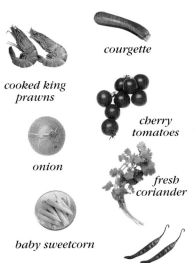

cooked king prawns

courgette

cherry tomatoes

onion

fresh coriander

baby sweetcorn

green chillies

salt

lemon juice

olive oil

1 To make the marinade, blend the coriander, salt, chillies, lemon juice and oil together in a food processor.

2 Empty the contents from the processor into a bowl.

NUTRITIONAL NOTES
PER PORTION:

ENERGY 95 Kcals/401 KJ
FAT 0.9 g **SATURATED FAT** 0.2 g
CHOLESTEROL 156 mg
FIBRE 0.9 g

3 Add the peeled king prawns to the mixture in the bowl and stir to make sure that all the prawns are well coated. Cover the bowl with clear film and set aside in a cool place to marinate for about 30 minutes.

4 Arrange the vegetables and prawns alternately on four long skewers. Cook on a medium barbecue for 5 minutes, turning frequently, until cooked and browned. Serve immediately, on a bed of mixed salad leaves.

Monkfish with Peppered Citrus Marinade

Monkfish is a firm, meaty fish that cooks well on the barbecue and keeps its shape. Serve with a green salad.

NUTRITIONAL NOTES
Per portion:

ENERGY 136 Kcals/574 KJ
FAT 3.8 g **SATURATED FAT** 0.6 g
CHOLESTEROL 22 mg
FIBRE 0

Serves 4

INGREDIENTS
2 monkfish tails, about 300 g/
    11 oz each
1 lime
1 lemon
2 oranges
handful of fresh thyme sprigs
30 ml/2 tbsp olive oil
15 ml/1 tbsp mixed peppercorns,
    roughly crushed
salt and freshly ground black pepper

monkfish tails

lime

oranges

lemon

mixed peppercorns

fresh thyme

olive oil

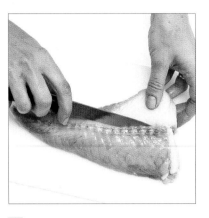

1 Remove any skin from the monkfish tails. Cut carefully down one side of the backbone, sliding the knife between the bone and flesh, to remove the fillet on one side.

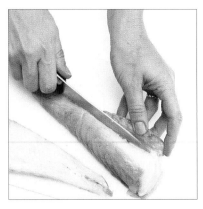

2 Turn the fish and repeat on the other side, to remove the second fillet. Repeat on the second tail. (You could ask your fishmonger to do this for you.) Lay the four fillets out flat.

3 Cut two slices from each of the citrus fruits and arrange them over two of the fillets. Add a few sprigs of thyme and sprinkle with salt and pepper. Finely grate the rind from the remaining fruit and sprinkle it over the fish.

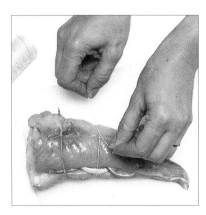

4 Lay the other two fillets on top and tie them firmly at intervals, with fine cotton string, to hold them in shape. Place in a wide dish.

5 Squeeze the juice from the remaining fruits. Mix with the oil and more salt and pepper. Spoon over the fish. Cover and leave to marinate for 1 hour in a cool place, turning a few times and spooning the marinade over it.

6 Drain the monkfish, reserving the marinade, and sprinkle with the crushed peppercorns. Cook on a medium-hot barbecue for 15–20 minutes, basting with the marinade and turning occasionally, until evenly cooked.

Marrakesh Monkfish with Chermoula

Chermoula is a Moroccan spice mixture, which is used as a marinade for meat, poultry and fish.

Serves 4

INGREDIENTS

1 small red onion, finely chopped
2 garlic cloves, crushed
1 fresh red chilli, seeded and
   finely chopped
30 ml/2 tbsp chopped fresh coriander
15 ml/1 tbsp chopped fresh mint
5 ml/1 tsp ground cumin
5 ml/1 tsp paprika
generous pinch of saffron strands
60 ml/4 tbsp olive oil
juice of 1 lemon
675 g/1½ lb monkfish fillets, skinned
salt
salad and pitta bread, to serve

red chilli
red onion
garlic
fresh coriander
fresh mint
ground cumin
paprika
saffron
olive oil
monkfish
lemon juice

1 To make the chermoula, mix the onion, garlic, chilli, coriander, mint, cumin, paprika, saffron, olive oil, lemon juice and salt together in a mixing bowl. Leave aside.

2 Cut the monkfish into cubes. Add them to the spice mixture in the bowl. Mix well to coat, cover and leave in a cool place for 1 hour.

3 Thread the monkfish on to skewers and place on the rack over a medium-hot barbecue. Spoon over a little of the marinade. Grill the monkfish skewers for about 3 minutes on each side, until cooked through and lightly browned. Serve with salad and warm pitta bread.

COOK'S TIP

If you use bamboo or wooden skewers, soak them in cold water for about 30 minutes before draining and threading them. This will help to prevent the skewers from scorching.

NUTRITIONAL NOTES

PER PORTION:

ENERGY 139 Kcals/590 KJ
FAT 3.2 g **SATURATED FAT** 0.5 g
CHOLESTEROL 24 mg
FIBRE 0.21 g

Jumbo Prawns with Salsa Verde and Lime

Limes are wonderfully versatile and look great simply cut into pieces, then sprinkled with a little finely chopped coriander or parsley.

Serves 4

INGREDIENTS
120 ml/4 fl oz/$\frac{1}{2}$ cup white wine
10 ml/2 tsp grated fresh root ginger
10 ml/2 tsp crushed garlic
24 raw jumbo prawns, peeled, with
    heads left on
2 limes and 15 ml/1 tbsp chopped
    fresh coriander, to garnish

FOR THE SALSA VERDE
1 small onion, quartered
1 bunch fresh coriander
5 ml/1 tsp crushed garlic
15 ml/1 tbsp olive oil

root ginger

onion

olive oil

garlic

fresh coriander

raw jumbo prawns

white wine

COOK'S TIP
Fresh ginger freezes well, wrapped in clear film or a plastic freezer bag. Dry ginger is not an acceptable substitute for fresh.

NUTRITIONAL NOTES
PER PORTION:

ENERGY 90 Kcals/384 KJ
FAT 2.8 g SATURATED FAT 0.5 g
CHOLESTEROL 183 mg
FIBRE 0.21 g

1 Combine the white wine, ginger and garlic in a medium bowl. Add the prawns, turning to coat them in the marinade. Cover and chill for 4–6 hours.

2 Make the salsa. Chop the onion coarsely in a food processor. Add the coriander and garlic and process until finely chopped. With the motor running, pour in the oil through the feeder tube of the processor. When the salsa is thick and creamy, scrape it into a serving bowl and leave aside.

3 Cook the prawns on a medium barbecue for 5–6 minutes, turning them once. Divide the prawns among four plates. Cut the limes in half lengthwise, then into wedges. Press the long edge of each wedge into the chopped fresh coriander. Place two wedges on each plate. Serve with the salsa verde.

Fish and Vegetable Kebabs

This can make an attractive main dish or a starter for eight. Serve it on a bed of flavoured or plain rice, if you like.

NUTRITIONAL NOTES
PER PORTION:

ENERGY 123 Kcals/612 KJ
FAT 3.5 g **SATURATED FAT** 0.6 g
CHOLESTEROL 154 mg
FIBRE 2.6 g

Serves 4

INGREDIENTS
275 g/10 oz cod fillets, or any other
   firm, white fish fillets
45 ml/3 tbsp lemon juice
5 ml/1 tsp grated fresh root ginger
2 fresh green chillies, very
   finely chopped
15 ml/1 tbsp very finely chopped
   fresh coriander
15 ml/1 tbsp very finely chopped
   fresh mint
5 ml/1 tsp ground coriander
5 ml/1 tsp salt
1 red pepper
1 green pepper
½ medium cauliflower
8–10 button mushrooms
8 cherry tomatoes
15 ml/1 tbsp vegetable oil
1 lime, quartered, to garnish

cod fillets
lemon juice
root ginger
green chillies
fresh coriander
fresh mint
ground coriander
salt
red pepper
green pepper
cauliflower
button mushrooms
cherry tomatoes
vegetable oil
lime

1 Using a sharp knife, cut the fish fillets into large, evenly sized chunks, (small ones would fall apart too easily and would disintegrate).

2 In a large mixing bowl, blend together the lemon juice, ginger, chopped green chillies, fresh coriander, mint, ground coriander and salt. Add the fish chunks and leave to marinate in a cool place for about 30 minutes.

3 Cut the red and green peppers into large squares and divide the cauliflower into individual florets.

4 Arrange the red and green peppers, cauliflower florets, mushrooms and cherry tomatoes alternately with the pieces of fish on four skewers.

5 Baste the kebabs with the oil and any remaining marinade. Grill over a medium-hot barbecue for about 7–10 minutes or until the fish is cooked right through. Garnish with the lime quarters and serve the kebabs either on their own or with rice.

Marinated Monkfish and Mussel Skewers

The marinade will make the monkfish both deliciously flavoured and quicker to barbecue, so observe the cooking time closely.

Serves 4

INGREDIENTS
450 g/1 lb monkfish, skinned
    and boned
5 ml/1 tsp olive oil
30 ml/2 tbsp lemon juice
5 ml/1 tsp paprika
1 garlic clove, crushed
4 turkey rashers
8 cooked mussels
8 large raw prawns
15 ml/1 tbsp chopped fresh dill
salt and freshly ground black pepper
lemon wedges, to garnish
salad and rice, to serve

mussels

turkey rashers

lemon juice

fresh dill

raw prawns

olive oil

paprika

garlic

monkfish

NUTRITIONAL NOTES
PER PORTION:

ENERGY 164 Kcals/695 KJ
FAT 2.2 g **SATURATED FAT** 0.5 g
CHOLESTEROL 91 mg
FIBRE 0

COOK'S TIP
If you thread your kebabs on to two parallel skewers they are easier to turn over.

1 Cut the monkfish into 2.5 cm/1 in cubes and place in a shallow glass dish. Mix together the oil, lemon juice, paprika, and garlic clove in a bowl and season with pepper.

2 Pour the marinade over the fish and toss to coat evenly. Cover and leave in a cool place for 30 minutes.

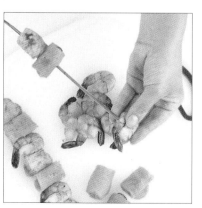

3 Cut the turkey rashers in half and wrap each strip around a mussel. Thread on to skewers alternating with the fish cubes and raw prawns.

4 Cook the kebabs over a hot barbecue for 7–8 minutes, turning once and basting with the marinade. Sprinkle with chopped dill and salt. Garnish with the lemon wedges and serve with salad and rice.

Baked Potatoes with Spicy Cottage Cheese

Always choose a variety of potato recommended for baking – this recipe requires that the texture of the potato should not be too dry.

NUTRITIONAL NOTES
PER PORTION:

ENERGY 311 Kcals/1449 KJ
FAT 3.6 g **SATURATED FAT** 0.75 g
CHOLESTEROL 2.5 mg
FIBRE 4.8 g

Serves 4

INGREDIENTS
4 medium baking potatoes
225 g/8 oz/1 cup low-fat
    cottage cheese
10 ml/2 tsp tomato purée
2.5 ml/½ tsp ground cumin
2.5 ml/½ tsp ground coriander
2.5 ml/½ tsp chilli powder
2.5 ml/½ tsp salt
15 ml/1 tbsp corn oil
2.5 ml/½ tsp mixed onion and
    mustard seeds
3 curry leaves
30 ml/2 tbsp water
mixed salad leaves, fresh coriander
    sprigs, lemon wedges and
    quartered tomatoes, to garnish

baking potatoes

low-fat cottage cheese

ground cumin

tomato purée

chilli powder

ground coriander

corn oil

curry leaves

salt

VARIATION

Jacket potatoes make a delicious vegetarian alternative to barbecued meat and fish. They are naturally low in fat and are full of energy as they are very high in carbohydrates. They are also extremely versatile and you can eat them with any topping.

1 Wash the potatoes, pat dry and make a slit in the middle of each one. Prick the potatoes a few times with a fork, then wrap them individually in foil. Cook over a medium-hot barbecue for about 1 hour, until soft.

2 Transfer the cottage cheese to a dish and set aside. In a separate bowl, mix together the tomato purée, ground cumin, ground coriander, chilli powder and salt.

3 Heat the corn oil in a small saucepan for 1 minute. Add the mixed onion and mustard seeds and the curry leaves, and make sure they are covered with the oil. When the leaves become dark, add the tomato purée mixture and lower the heat. Add the water and mix.

4 Cook for a further 1 minute, then pour the spicy tomato mixture on to the cottage cheese and blend everything together well.

5 Unwrap the cooked potatoes and divide the cottage cheese equally between them. Garnish with mixed salad leaves, fresh coriander sprigs, lemon wedges and tomato quarters.

Sweet and Sour Vegetables with Tofu

The marinade for these kebabs is a honey and chilli seasoned oil that makes a delicious contrast with the vegetable and fruit selection. It creates a truly sweet and sour flavour.

Serves 4

INGREDIENTS
1 green pepper, cut into squares
1 yellow pepper, cut into squares
8 cherry, or 4 medium, tomatoes
8 cauliflower florets
8 fresh or canned pineapple chunks
8 cubes tofu
boiled rice, to serve (optional)

FOR THE MARINADE
15 ml/1 tbsp vegetable oil
30 ml/2 tbsp lemon juice
5 ml/1 tsp salt
5 ml/1 tsp freshly ground
    black pepper
15 ml/1 tbsp clear honey
30 ml/2 tbsp chilli sauce

tofu   *yellow pepper*

cherry tomatoes

cauliflower

vegetable oil   *lemon juice*   *pineapple*

green pepper

salt   *black pepper*

clear honey   *chilli sauce*

NUTRITIONAL NOTES
PER PORTION:

ENERGY 75 Kcals/318 KJ
FAT 2.6 g SATURATED FAT 0.4 g
CHOLESTEROL 0
FIBRE 2.1 g

1 Thread the prepared vegetables, pineapple and tofu cubes on to four skewers, alternating the ingredients.

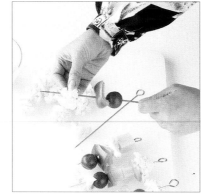

2 Prepare the marinade. Mix together all the ingredients. If the mixture is a little too thick, add 15 ml/1 tbsp water to dilute it a little.

3 Brush the skewers with the seasoned oil, ready for barbecuing. Cook on a hot barbecue for 10 minutes, until the vegetables begin to char slightly, turning the skewers often and basting with the seasoned oil. Serve on a bed of plain boiled rice, if you like.

Cassava and Vegetable Kebabs

This is an attractive and delicious assortment of African vegetables, marinated in a spicy garlic sauce. If cassava is unavailable, use sweet potato or yam. Serve with rice or couscous.

NUTRITIONAL NOTES

PER PORTION:

ENERGY 144 Kcals/610 KJ
FAT 3.3 g **SATURATED FAT** 0.5 g
CHOLESTEROL 0
FIBRE 2.7 g

Serves 4

INGREDIENTS
175 g/6 oz cassava
1 onion, cut into wedges
1 aubergine, cut into bite-size pieces
1 courgette, sliced
1 ripe plantain, sliced
1/2 red pepper, sliced
1/2 green pepper, sliced
16 cherry tomatoes
rice or couscous, to serve

FOR THE MARINADE
60 ml/4 tbsp lemon juice
60 ml/4 tbsp olive oil
45-60 ml/3-4 tbsp soy sauce
15 ml/1 tbsp tomato purée
1 green chilli, seeded and
    finely chopped
1/2 onion, grated
2 garlic cloves, crushed
5 ml/1 tsp mixed spice
pinch of dried thyme

1 Peel the cassava and cut into bite-size pieces. Place in a bowl, cover with boiling water and leave to blanch for 5 minutes. Drain well. Place all the vegetables and the cassava, (but not the cherry tomatoes) in a large bowl and mix with your hands to distribute all the vegetables evenly.

cassava

aubergine

courgettes

plantain

red pepper

green pepper

cherry tomatoes

lemon juice

olive oil

soy sauce

tomato purée

garlic cloves

onion

green chilli

mixed spice

dried thyme

2 Blend together all the marinade ingredients and pour over the vegetables. Set aside for 1-2 hours.

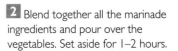

3 Thread all the vegetables and cherry tomatoes on to eight skewers. Cook on a hot barbecue for 15 minutes until tender, turning frequently and basting occasionally. Serve with rice or couscous.

Red Bean and Mushroom Burgers

Vegetarians and meat-eaters alike will enjoy these healthy, low-fat veggie burgers. Served with salad, pitta bread and Greek-style yogurt, they make a substantial meal.

NUTRITIONAL NOTES
PER PORTION:

ENERGY 128 Kcals/541 KJ
FAT 3.4 g **SATURATED FAT** 0.5 g
CHOLESTEROL 0
FIBRE 6.6 g

COOK'S TIP
These burgers are not quite as firm as meat burgers, and will need careful handling on the barbecue unless you use a wire rack.

Serves 4

INGREDIENTS
15 ml/1 tbsp olive oil, plus extra
    for brushing
1 small onion, finely chopped
1 garlic clove, crushed
5 ml/1 tsp ground cumin
5 ml/1 tsp ground coriander
2.5 ml/½ tsp ground turmeric
115 g/4 oz/1½ cups finely
    chopped mushrooms
400 g/14 oz can red kidney beans
30 ml/2 tbsp chopped fresh coriander
wholemeal flour
salt and freshly ground black pepper
low-fat Greek-style yogurt, pitta bread
    and salad, to serve

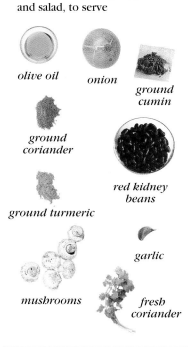

olive oil   *onion*

*ground
cumin*

*ground
coriander*

*red kidney
beans*

ground turmeric

garlic

mushrooms   *fresh
coriander*

1 Heat the olive oil in a frying pan and fry the chopped onion and garlic over a moderate heat, stirring, until softened. Add the spices and cook for 1 minute further, stirring continuously.

2 Add the chopped mushrooms and cook, stirring, until softened and the mixture has become dry. Remove the pan from the heat and empty the contents into a large bowl.

3 Drain the beans thoroughly, place them in a bowl and mash with a fork.

4 Stir the kidney beans into the frying pan, with the chopped fresh coriander, and mix thoroughly. Season the mixture well with plenty of salt and freshly ground black pepper.

5 Using floured hands, form the mixture into four flat burger shapes. If the mixture is too sticky to handle, mix in a little wholemeal flour.

6 Lightly brush the burgers with olive oil and cook on a hot barbecue for 8–10 minutes, turning once, until golden brown. Serve with a spoonful of yogurt, pitta bread and a green salad, if liked.

Herb Polenta with Grilled Tomatoes

This recipe combines golden polenta with fresh summer herbs and sweet grilled tomatoes.

Serves 4

INGREDIENTS
750 ml/1¼ pints/3 cups vegetable
   stock or water
5 ml/1 tsp salt
175 g/6 oz/1 cup polenta
10 g/¼ oz/2 tsp butter
75 ml/5 tbsp mixed chopped fresh
   parsley, chives and basil, plus
   extra, to garnish
5 ml/1 tsp olive oil
4 large plum or beef tomatoes, halved
salt and freshly ground black pepper

stock

salt

olive oil

plum tomatoes

butter

polenta

fresh basil

fresh parsley

fresh chives

NUTRITIONAL NOTES
PER PORTION:

ENERGY 185 Kcals/775 KJ
FAT 4.3 g SATURATED FAT 1.49 g
CHOLESTEROL 0
FIBRE 0.5 g

1 Prepare the polenta in advance: place the water or stock in a pan, with the salt, and bring to the boil. Reduce the heat and stir in the polenta.

2 Stir constantly over a moderate heat for 5 minutes, until the polenta begins to thicken and come away from the sides of the pan.

COOK'S TIP

Any mixture of fresh herbs can be used, or try using just basil or chives alone for a really distinctive flavour.

3 Remove from the heat and stir in the butter, herbs and black pepper.

4 Lightly grease a wide dish, add the polenta and spread out evenly. Once set, turn out and cut into shapes. Brush the tomatoes and polenta with oil and season. Cook on a medium-hot barbecue for 5 minutes, turning once. Serve garnished with fresh herbs.

Tofu Steaks

These tofu steaks are so full of Japanese flavour, they will please even the most committed meat-eater. They cook quickly, too.

Serves 4

INGREDIENTS
1 packet fresh tofu (10 x 8 x 3 cm/
   4 x 3¼ x 1¼ in), 300 g/11 oz
   drained weight
2 spring onions, thinly sliced,
   to garnish
mixed salad leaves, to garnish

FOR THE MARINADE
45 ml/3 tbsp sake
30 ml/2 tbsp soy sauce
5 ml/1 tsp sesame oil
1 garlic clove, crushed
15 ml/1 tbsp grated fresh root ginger
1 spring onion, finely chopped

tofu

spring onions

sake

soy sauce

sesame oil

garlic

root ginger

NUTRITIONAL NOTES
PER PORTION:

ENERGY 59 Kcals/246 KJ
FAT 3.6 g SATURATED FAT 0.4 g
CHOLESTEROL 0
FIBRE 0

1 Wrap the tofu in a clean tea towel and place between two plates. Leave the tofu aside for 30 minutes to remove any excess water.

2 Slice the tofu horizontally into 12 steaks. Set aside. Mix the ingredients for the marinade in a large bowl. Add the tofu to the bowl in a single layer and allow to marinate for 30 minutes. Drain the tofu steaks and reserve the marinade to use for basting.

3 Cook the steaks on a hot barbecue for 3 minutes on each side, basting regularly with the marinade.

4 Arrange three tofu steaks on each plate. Any remaining marinade can be heated in a pan and then poured over the steaks. Sprinkle with the spring onions and garnish with mixed salad leaves. Serve immediately.

COOK'S TIP
Tofu is easily obtainable from supermarkets and health food stores, and is an ideal alternative to meat.

Summer Vegetables with Yogurt Pesto

Char-grilled vegetables make a meal on their own, or are delicious served as a Mediterranean-style accompaniment to grilled meats and fish.

Serves 4

INGREDIENTS
2 small aubergines
2 large courgettes
1 red pepper
1 yellow pepper
1 fennel bulb
1 red onion
10 ml/2 tsp olive oil
salt and freshly ground black pepper

FOR THE YOGURT PESTO
150 ml/¼ pint/⅔ cup fat-free Greek-style yogurt
15 ml/1 tbsp pesto

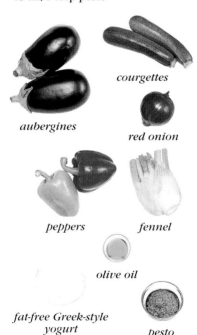

courgettes

aubergines

red onion

peppers   *fennel*

olive oil

fat-free Greek-style yogurt   *pesto*

1 Cut the aubergines into 1 cm/½ in slices. Sprinkle with salt and leave to drain for about 30 minutes. Rinse well in cold running water and pat dry.

2 Use a sharp kitchen knife to cut the courgettes in half lengthways. Cut the peppers in half, removing the seeds but leaving the stalks intact.

3 Slice the fennel bulb and the red onion into thick wedges, using a sharp kitchen knife.

4 Stir the yogurt and pesto lightly together in a serving bowl, to make a marbled sauce. Set aside.

5 Arrange the vegetables on the hot barbecue, brush with the olive oil and sprinkle with plenty of salt and freshly ground black pepper.

6 Cook the vegetables until golden brown and tender, turning occasionally. The aubergines and peppers will take 6–8 minutes to cook, and the courgettes, onion and fennel will take 4–5 minutes. Serve the vegetables immediately, with the yogurt pesto.

Vegetable Kebabs with Mustard and Honey

A colourful mixture of vegetables and tofu, skewered, glazed and grilled until tender.

NUTRITIONAL NOTES
PER PORTION:

ENERGY 202 Kcals/855 KJ
FAT 0.47 g SATURATED FAT 0.77 g
CHOLESTEROL 0
FIBRE 1.4 g

Serves 4

INGREDIENTS
1 yellow pepper
2 small courgettes
225 g/8 oz piece firm tofu
8 cherry tomatoes
8 button mushrooms
15 ml/1 tbsp wholegrain mustard
15 ml/1 tbsp clear honey
30 ml/2 tbsp olive oil
salt and freshly ground black pepper
lime segments and flat leaf parsley,
    to garnish
rice, to serve (optional)

courgettes

cherry tomatoes

clear honey

yellow pepper

tofu

olive oil

wholegrain mustard

button mushrooms

1 Cut the pepper in half and remove the seeds. Cut each half into eight.

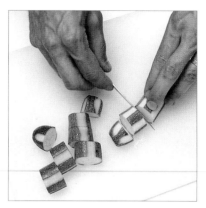

2 Top and tail the courgettes and peel them decoratively, if you like. Cut each courgette into eight chunks.

3 Rinse the tofu under cold running water and drain well. Cut the tofu into neat, square pieces of a similar size to the vegetables.

4 Thread the pepper pieces, courgette chunks, tofu, cherry tomatoes and mushrooms alternately on to four metal or wooden skewers.

5 Whisk the mustard, honey and olive oil in a small bowl. Add salt and pepper to taste.

6 Brush the kebabs with the mustard and honey glaze. Cook over a hot barbecue for eight minutes, turning once or twice during cooking. Serve with a mixture of long grain and wild rice, if you like, and garnish with lime segments and parsley.

Summer Pasta Salad

Tender young vegetables with pasta in a light dressing make a delicious accompaniment to barbecued chicken or fish.

Serves 4

INGREDIENTS
225 g/8 oz fusilli or other dried
    pasta shapes
115 g/4 oz baby carrots, trimmed
    and halved
115 g/4 oz baby sweetcorn,
    halved lengthways
50 g/2 oz mangetouts
115 g/4 oz young asparagus
    spears, trimmed
4 spring onions, trimmed
    and shredded
10 ml/2 tsp white wine vinegar
10 ml/2 tsp olive oil
15 ml/1 tbsp wholegrain mustard
salt and freshly ground black pepper

spring onions

fusilli

young asparagus

wholegrain mustard

baby carrots

baby sweetcorn

white wine vinegar

mangetouts

olive oil

1 Bring a large pan of salted water to the boil. Add the pasta and cook for 10–12 minutes, until just tender. Meanwhile, cook the carrots and sweetcorn in a second pan of boiling salted water for 5 minutes.

2 Add the mangetouts and asparagus to the carrot mixture and cook for about 2–3 minutes more. Drain all the vegetables and refresh under cold running water. Drain again.

3 Tip the vegetable mixture into a bowl, add the spring onions and toss.

NUTRITIONAL NOTES

PER PORTION:

ENERGY 238 Kcals/1009 KJ
FAT 3.2 g **SATURATED FAT** 0.4 g
CHOLESTEROL 0
FIBRE 3.75 g

4 Drain the pasta, refresh it under cold running water and drain again. Toss with the vegetables. Mix the vinegar, olive oil and mustard in a jar. Add salt and pepper to taste, close the jar tightly and shake well. Pour the dressing over the salad. Toss well and serve.

Marinated Cucumber Salad

Sprinkling the cucumbers with salt draws out some of the water and makes them less bitter.

Serves 4

INGREDIENTS
2 medium cucumbers
15 ml/1 tbsp salt
90 g/3½ oz/½ cup granulated sugar
175 ml/6 fl oz/⅔ cup dry cider
15 ml/1 tbsp cider vinegar
45 ml/3 tbsp chopped fresh dill
pinch of pepper

dry cider

granulated sugar

fresh dill

cucumbers

cider vinegar

salt

1 Slice the cucumbers thinly and place them in a colander, sprinkling salt between each layer. Put the colander over a bowl and leave to drain for about 1 hour.

2 Thoroughly rinse the cucumber under cold running water to remove excess salt, then pat dry with absorbent kitchen paper.

COOK'S TIP

Try to eat this salad while it is as fresh as possible, as the vinegar will make the cucumber soft and discoloured if left too long.

3 Gently heat the sugar, cider and vinegar in a saucepan, until the sugar has dissolved. Remove from the heat and leave to cool. Put the cucumber slices in a bowl, pour over the cider mixture and leave to marinate for 2 hours.

4 Drain the cucumber and sprinkle with the dill and pepper to taste. Mix well and transfer to a serving dish. Chill in the fridge until ready to serve.

Fruity Rice Salad

This appetizing and colourful rice salad, combining many different flavours, is ideal for a barbecue.

Serves 4

INGREDIENTS

225 g/8 oz/1 cup mixed brown and wild rice
1 yellow pepper, seeded and diced
1 bunch spring onions, chopped
3 celery sticks, chopped
1 large beef tomato, chopped
2 green-skinned eating apples, chopped
175 g/6 oz/³/₄ cup ready-to-eat dried apricots, chopped
115 g/4 oz/²/₃ cup raisins
30 ml/2 tbsp unsweetened apple juice
30 ml/2 tbsp dry sherry
30 ml/2 tbsp light soy sauce
dash of Tabasco sauce
30 ml/2 tbsp chopped fresh parsley
15 ml/1 tbsp chopped fresh rosemary
salt and freshly ground black pepper

mixed brown and wild rice   *yellow pepper*   *beef tomato*   *dried apricots*

spring onions   *eating apples*   *Tabasco sauce*   *fresh parsley*   *fresh rosemary*

raisins   *celery*   *soy sauce*

apple juice   *dry sherry*

NUTRITIONAL NOTES

PER PORTION:

ENERGY 420 Kcals/1787 KJ
FAT 2.4 g **SATURATED FAT** 0.4 g
CHOLESTEROL 0
FIBRE 7.3g

1 Cook the rice in a large saucepan of lightly salted, boiling water for about 30 minutes (or according to the instructions on the packet) until tender. Rinse the rice under cold running water to cool quickly then drain thoroughly.

2 Place the pepper, spring onions, celery, tomato, apples, apricots, raisins and the cooked rice in a serving bowl and mix well.

3 Now make the dressing. In a small bowl, mix together the apple juice, dry sherry, soy sauce, Tabasco sauce, chopped fresh parsley, chopped fresh rosemary, salt and freshly ground black pepper.

4 Pour the salad dressing over the prepared rice, vegetable and fruit mixture. Toss all the ingredients together gently but thoroughly. Serve immediately, or cover and chill in the fridge for 1–2 hours before serving.

Bulgur Wheat and Mint Salad

Also known as cracked wheat, burghul or pourgouri, bulgur wheat has already been partially cooked, so it requires only a short period of soaking before serving.

Serves 4

INGREDIENTS

250 g/9 oz/1²/₃ cups bulgur wheat
4 tomatoes, chopped
4 small courgettes, thinly
    sliced lengthways
4 spring onions, sliced on
    the diagonal
8 ready-to-eat dried apricots, chopped
40 g/1¹/₂ oz/¹/₄ cup raisins
juice of 1 lemon
30 ml/2 tbsp tomato juice
45 ml/3 tbsp chopped fresh mint
1 garlic clove, crushed
salt and freshly ground black pepper
sprig of fresh mint, to garnish

dried apricots

raisins

courgettes

spring onions

tomatoes

lemon juice

tomato juice

fresh mint

bulgur wheat

garlic

1 Put the bulgur wheat into a large bowl. Add enough cold water to come 2.5 cm/1 in above the surface of the wheat. Leave to soak for 30 minutes, then drain well and squeeze out any excess water in a clean tea towel.

2 Meanwhile, plunge the tomatoes into boiling water and leave for 1 minute. Then plunge into cold water. Remove the skins, which should now slip off easily. Halve the tomatoes, remove the seeds and cores, and roughly chop the flesh.

3 Now add the tomatoes, courgettes, spring onions, apricots and raisins to the soaked and drained bulgur wheat. Stir well but gently until the ingredients are thoroughly combined.

4 Put the lemon and tomato juice, mint, garlic and seasoning into a small bowl and whisk together with a fork. Pour over the salad and mix well. Chill in the fridge for at least 1 hour. Serve garnished with a sprig of mint.

COOK'S TIP

Bulgur wheat is made from wholewheat grain, including the wheat germ, and is a rich source of nutrients. It has a distinctive flavour and can be used in a variety of dishes.

NUTRITIONAL NOTES

PER PORTION:

ENERGY 227 Kcals/956 KJ
FAT 1.27 g **SATURATED FAT** 0.1 g
CHOLESTEROL 0
FIBRE 2.9 g

Watercress and Potato Salad

New potatoes are equally good hot or cold, and this colourful, nutritious salad is an ideal way to make the most of them. Everyone loves a potato salad with their barbecue.

Serves 4

INGREDIENTS
450 g/1 lb small new
    potatoes, unpeeled
1 bunch watercress
225 g/8 oz cherry tomatoes, halved
30 ml/2 tbsp pumpkin seeds
45 ml/3 tbsp fat-free fromage frais
15 ml/1 tbsp cider vinegar
5 ml/1 tsp soft brown sugar
salt and paprika

new potatoes

watercress

brown sugar

pumpkin seeds

cherry tomatoes

fat-free fromage frais

cider vinegar

NUTRITIONAL NOTES
PER PORTION:

ENERGY 146 Kcals/618 KJ
FAT 4.4 g **SATURATED FAT** 0.8 g
CHOLESTEROL 0
FIBRE 3.2 g

1 Cook the new potatoes over a low heat in lightly salted, boiling water for about 20–30 minutes, depending on their size, until just tender. Then drain them and leave to cool.

COOK'S TIP
New potatoes are delicious cooked and eaten with their skins still on. Some people, however, don't like the skins, in which case you should cook them with the skins on and then peel them when they have cooled. Serve this salad at room temperature.

2 Toss together the potatoes, watercress, tomatoes and pumpkin seeds in a mixing bowl.

3 Place the fromage frais, vinegar, sugar, salt and paprika in a screw-top jar and shake well to mix. Pour over the salad just before serving.

Fennel and Herb Coleslaw

The addition of fennel to this coleslaw gives it a distinctive anise flavour which pairs well with grilled meat. There is no mayonnaise in this salad but it is just as flavoursome without as well as being much lighter and healthier.

Serves 4

INGREDIENTS
1 fennel bulb
2 spring onions
$\frac{1}{2}$ white cabbage
2 celery sticks
3 carrots
50 g/2 oz sultanas
2.5 ml/$\frac{1}{2}$ tsp caraway
    seeds (optional)
15 ml/1 tbsp chopped fresh parsley
15 ml/1 tbsp olive oil
5 ml/1 tsp lemon juice
shreds of spring onion, to garnish

fennel

spring onions

white cabbage

sultanas

lemon juice

celery

carrots

fresh parsley

olive oil

1 Using a really sharp knife, cut the fennel bulbs into thin slices. Then also slice the spring onions finely. Put to one side for use later.

2 Slice the cabbage and celery finely and cut the carrots into julienne strips. Place in a serving bowl together with the other vegetables.

3 Add the sultanas and caraway seeds, if using. Stir in the chopped parsley, olive oil and lemon juice and mix well. Cover and chill for 3 hours to allow the flavours to mingle. Serve, garnished with the spring onion shreds.

COOK'S TIP
The best olive oil that you can use is extra virgin olive oil.

NUTRITIONAL NOTES
PER PORTION:

ENERGY 94 Kcals/397 KJ
FAT 3.2 g SATURATED FAT 0.4 g
CHOLESTEROL 0
FIBRE 3.7 g

Mango, Tomato and Red Onion Salad

The under-ripe mango has a subtle sweetness that blends well with the tomato.

Serves 4

INGREDIENTS
1 firm under-ripe mango
2 large tomatoes or 1 beef
    tomato, sliced
1/2 red onion, sliced into rings
1/2 cucumber, peeled and thinly sliced
15 ml/1 tbsp sunflower or
    vegetable oil
15 ml/1 tbsp lemon juice
1 garlic clove, crushed
2.5 ml/1/2 tsp hot pepper sauce
sugar, to taste
salt and freshly ground black pepper
snipped chives, to garnish

mango

tomatoes

red onion

cucumber

garlic

hot pepper sauce

oil

lemon juice

sugar

1 Cut away two thick slices from either side of the mango stone and cut into smaller slices. Peel the skin from the slices. Arrange the mango, tomato, onion and cucumber slices in a decorative design on a serving plate.

VARIATION

Slices of avocado would make a delicious alternative to the mango. However, avocados have a very high oil content, so don't try this if you are on a low-fat diet!

NUTRITIONAL NOTES
PER PORTION:

ENERGY 57 Kcals/241 KJ
FAT 2.9 g **SATURATED FAT** 0.3 g
CHOLESTEROL 0
FIBRE 1.6 g

2 Blend the oil, lemon juice, garlic, hot pepper sauce, salt and black pepper in a blender or food processor, or place in a small jar and shake vigorously. Add a pinch of sugar to taste and mix again.

3 Pour the dressing over the salad and garnish with the snipped chives.

Fattoush

This simple peasant salad is a popular dish all over Syria and the Lebanon. It will complement the flavours of any barbecue party.

Serves 4

INGREDIENTS
1 yellow or red pepper
1 large cucumber
4-5 tomatoes
1 bunch spring onions
30 ml/2 tbsp finely chopped
    fresh parsley
30 ml/2 tbsp finely chopped fresh
    mint
30 ml/2 tbsp finely chopped
    fresh coriander
2 garlic cloves, crushed
15 ml/1 tbsp olive oil
juice of 2 lemons
salt and freshly ground black pepper
2 pitta breads, to serve

pepper

cucumber

fresh parsley

spring onions

fresh coriander

tomatoes

lemon juice

olive oil

garlic

fresh mint

1 Halve and core the pepper, discarding the seeds, and slice it thinly. Coarsely chop the cucumber and tomatoes. Place the pepper, cucumber and tomatoes in a large salad bowl.

2 Trim and slice the spring onions. Add to the pepper, cucumber and tomatoes with the finely chopped parsley, mint and coriander.

3 To make the dressing, blend the garlic, olive oil and lemon juice together, then season to taste with salt and black pepper.

VARIATION

After toasting the pitta bread until crisp, crush it in your hand and sprinkle it over the salad before serving, for a more traditional touch.

NUTRITIONAL NOTES
PER PORTION:

ENERGY 164 Kcals/696 KJ
FAT 3.8 g SATURATED FAT 0.5 g
CHOLESTEROL 0
FIBRE 4.3 g

COOK'S TIP

If you have plenty of herbs to hand, you can add as many as you like to this aromatic salad.

4 Pour the dressing over the salad and toss lightly to mix. Toast the pitta bread on the barbecue until crisp and serve it with the salad.

Pineapple Wedges with Allspice and Lime

Fresh pineapple is easy to prepare and always looks very attractive, so this dish is perfect for easy outdoor entertaining.

Serves 4

INGREDIENTS
1 medium-size, ripe pineapple
1 lime
15 ml/1 tbsp dark muscovado sugar
5 ml/1 tsp ground allspice

ground allspice

pineapple

dark muscovado sugar

lime

1 Cut the pineapple lengthways into quarters and remove the core.

2 Slice the flesh away from the skin. Cut into slices and arrange decoratively upon the skin.

VARIATION

For a hot dish, place the pineapple slices on a wire rack, sprinkle them with the lime juice, sugar and allspice, and place them on a hot barbecue for 3-4 minutes until golden and bubbling. Sprinkle with shreds of lime zest and serve.

NUTRITIONAL NOTES
PER PORTION:

ENERGY 55 Kcals/231 KJ
FAT 0.2 g **SATURATED FAT** 0
CHOLESTEROL 0
FIBRE 1.1 g

3 Remove a few shreds of rind from the lime and then squeeze out the juice.

4 Sprinkle the pineapple with the lime juice and rind, sugar and allspice. Serve immediately, or chill for up to an hour.

Baked Bananas with Spicy Vanilla Butter

Baked bananas are a must for the barbecue – they're so easy because they bake in their own skins and need no preparation at all. A flavoured butter melting over them adds richness, or you can use jam or honey.

Serves 4

INGREDIENTS
4 bananas
6 green cardamom pods
1 vanilla pod
finely grated rind of 1 small orange
30 ml/2 tbsp brandy or orange juice
60 ml/4 tbsp light muscovado sugar
20 ml/4 tsp butter
crème fraîche or low-fat Greek-style
    yogurt, to serve

brandy   *butter*

orange

bananas

*green cardamom
pods*

vanilla pod   *light muscovado
sugar*

NUTRITIONAL NOTES
PER PORTION:

ENERGY 177 Kcals/751 KJ
FAT 4.4 g **SATURATED FAT** 2.9 g
CHOLESTEROL 10.1 mg
FIBRE 0.9 g

1 Place the bananas, in their skins, on the hot barbecue and leave for about 6–8 minutes, turning occasionally, until they are turning brownish-black.

2 Meanwhile, split the cardamom pods and remove the seeds. Crush lightly in a pestle and mortar.

3 Split the vanilla pod lengthways and scrape out the tiny seeds. Mix with the cardamom seeds, orange rind, brandy or juice, sugar and butter, into a thick paste.

4 Slit the skin of each banana, open out slightly and spoon in a little of the paste. Serve with a spoonful of crème fraîche or Greek-style yogurt.

Baked Apples in Honey and Lemon

Tender baked apples with a classic flavouring of lemon and honey make a simple dessert for cooking on the barbecue. Serve with custard or a spoonful of low-fat yogurt, if liked.

Serves 4

INGREDIENTS
4 medium cooking apples
15 ml/1 tbsp clear honey
grated rind and juice of 1 lemon
15 ml/1 tbsp butter, melted

lemon

cooking apples

butter

clear honey

1 Remove the cores from the apples, leaving them whole. Cut four squares of double-thickness baking foil, to wrap the apples. Brush the foil with butter.

2 Using a cannelle or sharp knife, cut vertical lines through the surface of the apple skin at regular intervals.

3 Mix together the honey, lemon rind, juice and butter in a small bowl.

4 Spoon the mixture into the apples and wrap in foil, sealing the edges securely. Cook on a hot barbecue for 20 minutes, until the apples are tender.

Frudités with Honey Dip

A luscious dessert consisting of a selection of fresh summer fruits, this is simply delicious. It makes an equally delicious breakfast.

Serves 4

INGREDIENTS
250 ml/8 fl oz/1 cup low-fat
    Greek-style yogurt
45ml/3 tbsp clear honey
selection of fresh fruit for dipping
    such as apples, tangerines, grapes,
    figs, plums and strawberries

low-fat Greek-style yogurt

clear honey

apples

plums

grapes

tangerines

strawberries

figs

1 Place the yogurt in a dish, beat until smooth, then stir in the honey, leaving a little marbled effect.

2 Prepare the fruit pieces. Peel the tangerines and divide the segments. Cut the plums in half, remove the stones and halve again.

NUTRITIONAL NOTES

PER PORTION OF DIP:

ENERGY 67.5 Kcals/285 KJ
FAT 0.5 g **SATURATED FAT** 0.3 g
CHOLESTEROL 2.5 mg
FIBRE 0

3 Cut the rest of the fruits into wedges or bite-sized pieces, or leave some whole.

4 Arrange the fresh fruit on a platter with the bowl of honey dip in the centre. Serve chilled.

Papaya Skewers with a Passion Fruit Coulis

Tropical fruits, full of natural sweetness, make a simple, exotic dessert.

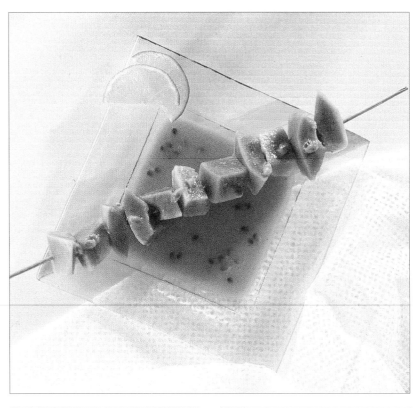

Serves 6

INGREDIENTS
3 ripe papayas
10 passion fruit or kiwi fruit
30 ml/2 tbsp lime juice
30 ml/2 tbsp icing sugar
30 ml/2 tbsp white rum
lime slices, to garnish

icing sugar

white rum

papayas

passion fruit

lime

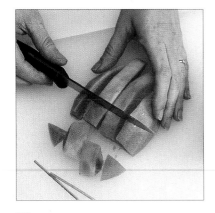

1 Cut the papayas in half and scoop out the seeds. Peel them and cut the flesh into evenly sized chunks. Thread the chunks on to six skewers.

2 Halve eight of the passion fruit or kiwi fruit and scoop out the flesh. Purée the flesh for a few seconds in a blender or food processor.

3 Press the pulp through a sieve and discard the seeds. Add the lime juice, icing sugar and rum, then stir well.

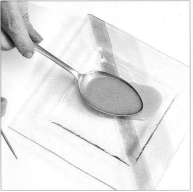

4 When the sugar has dissolved in the mixture, spoon a little coulis on to six serving plates. Place the skewers on top. Scoop the flesh from the remaining passion fruit or kiwi fruit and spoon it over the top. Garnish with lime slices and serve.

COOK'S TIP

If you are short of time, the passion fruit flesh can be used as it is, without puréeing or sieving. Simply scoop the flesh from the skins and mix it with the lime, sugar and rum. The kiwi fruit will still need to be puréed, however.

NUTRITIONAL NOTES
PER PORTION:

ENERGY 151 Kcals/643 KJ
FAT 0.8 g **SATURATED FAT** 0
CHOLESTEROL 0
FIBRE 4.9 g

Passion Fruit and Raspberry Swirls

If passion fruit is not available, this simple dessert can be made with raspberries alone. It is absolutely delicious served chilled on a warm day.

Serves 4

INGREDIENTS
550 ml/2¼ cups raspberries
2 passion fruit
400 ml/14 fl oz/1⅔ cups fat-free
    fromage frais
30 ml/2 tbsp white sugar
4 raspberries and sprigs of mint,
    to decorate

raspberries   *passion fruit*

*fat-free
fromage frais*   *white sugar*

1 Mash the raspberries in a small bowl until the juice runs.

2 Scoop out the passion fruit pulp into a separate bowl with the fromage frais and sugar and mix well.

COOK'S TIP
Over-ripe, slightly soft fruit can also be used in this recipe. Use frozen raspberries when fresh ones are not available, but thaw first.

3 Spoon alternate spoonfuls of the raspberry pulp and the fromage frais mixture into stemmed glasses or one large serving dish.

4 Stir the pulp lightly, to create a swirled effect. Decorate each dessert with a whole raspberry and a sprig of fresh mint. Leave in the fridge to chill until ready to serve.

Fruit Crush with Fruit Kebabs

Fruit crush is just the answer on a sultry summer's day, served with mouthwatering fruit kebabs.

NUTRITIONAL NOTES
Per portion:

ENERGY 216 Kcals/924 KJ
FAT 0.4 g **SATURATED FAT** 0.03 g
CHOLESTEROL 0
FIBRE 1.2 g

Serves 6

INGREDIENTS
FOR THE FRUIT CRUSH
300 ml/¹/₂ pint/1¹/₄ cups orange juice
300 ml/¹/₂ pint/1¹/₄ cups pineapple juice
300 ml/¹/₂ pint/1¹/₄ cups tropical fruit juice
475 ml/16 fl oz/2 cups lemonade
fresh pineapple slices and fresh cherries, to decorate

FOR THE FRUIT KEBABS
24 small strawberries
24 green seedless grapes
12 marshmallows
1 kiwi fruit, peeled and cut into 12 wedges
1 banana
15 ml/1 tbsp lemon juice

pineapple juice

kiwi fruit

lemon juice

lemonade

marshmallows

banana

green grapes

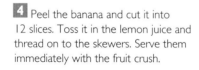
tropical fruit juice

orange juice

strawberries

1 To make the fruit crush, put the orange juice and the pineapple juice into ice-cube trays and freeze them until they have become solid.

4 Peel the banana and cut it into 12 slices. Toss it in the lemon juice and thread on to the skewers. Serve them immediately with the fruit crush.

2 Mix together the tropical fruit juice and lemonade in a large jug. Put a mixture of the ice cubes in each glass, pour the fruit crush over and decorate each glass with the pineapple slices and the cherries.

3 To make the fruit kebabs, thread two strawberries, two grapes, a marshmallow and a wedge of kiwi fruit on to each of the 12 wooden skewers.

Watermelon Sorbet

A slice of this colourful, tangy and refreshing sorbet is the perfect way to quench your thirst and cool down on a hot sunny day.

Serves 4-6

INGREDIENTS
½ small watermelon, weighing about
   1 kg/2¼ lb
75 g/3 oz/½ cup caster sugar
60 ml/4 tbsp cranberry juice or water
30 ml/2 tbsp lemon juice
sprigs of fresh mint, to decorate

cranberry juice

caster sugar

lemon juice

watermelon

COOK'S TIP
If preferred, this pretty pink sorbet can be served scooped into balls. Do this before the mixture is completely frozen and re-freeze the balls on a baking sheet until ready to serve.

1 Cut the watermelon into four to six equally sized wedges (depending on the number of servings you require). Scoop out the pink flesh, discarding the seeds but reserving the shell.

2 Line a freezer-proof bowl, about the same size as the melon, with clear film. Arrange the melon skins in the bowl to re-form the shell, fitting them together snugly so that there are no gaps. Put in the freezer.

3 Put the sugar and cranberry juice or water in a saucepan and stir over a low heat until the sugar dissolves. Bring to the boil and simmer for 5 minutes. Leave the sugar syrup to cool.

4 Put the melon flesh and lemon juice in a blender and process to a smooth purée. Stir in the sugar syrup and pour into a freezer-proof container. Freeze for 3–3½ hours, or until slushy.

5 Tip the sorbet into a chilled bowl and whisk to break up the ice crystals. Return to the freezer for another 30 minutes, whisk again, then tip into the melon shell and freeze until solid.

6 Remove from the freezer and leave to defrost at room temperature for 15 minutes. Take the melon out of the bowl and cut into wedges with a sharp, warmed knife. Decorate with sprigs of fresh mint and serve.

NUTRITIONAL NOTES
PER PORTION:

ENERGY 118 Kcals/507 KJ
FAT 0.5 g **SATURATED FAT** 0
CHOLESTEROL 0
FIBRE 0.25 g

INDEX